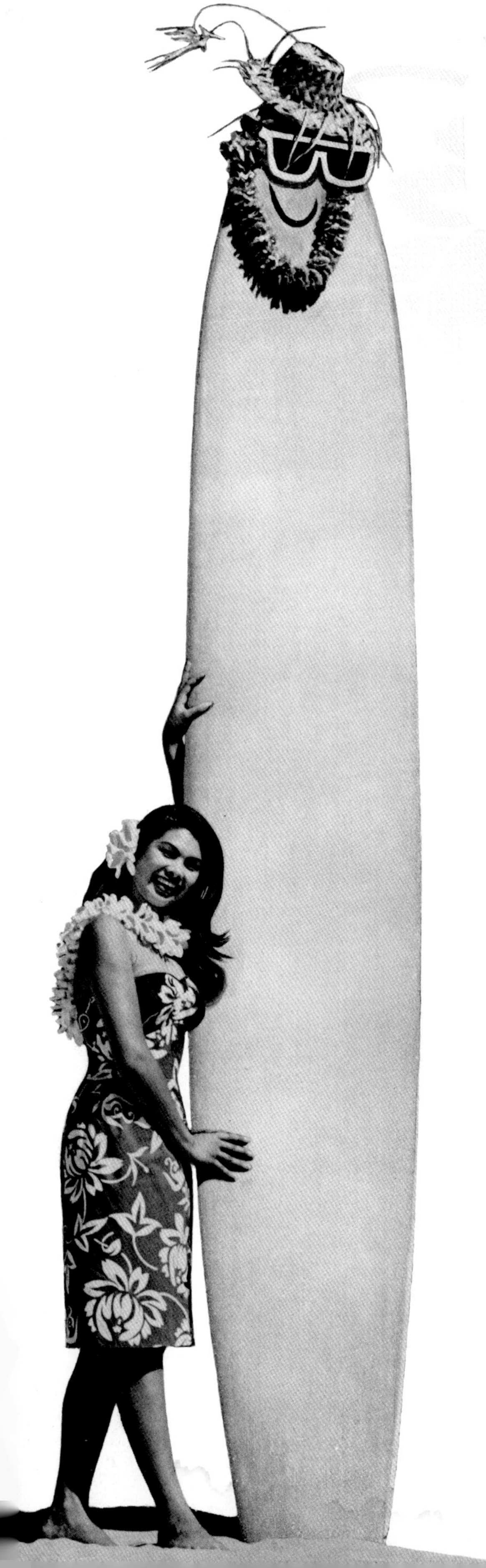

SURFING

SURFING

Historic Images from Bishop Museum Archives

by DeSoto Brown

BISHOP MUSEUM PRESS
Honolulu, Hawai i

Copyright © 2006 by Bishop Museum

All rights reserved. No part of this book may be reproduced or transmitted in any form or by any means, electronic, mechanical, digital including photocopying, recording, or by any information storage and retrieval system, without prior written permission from the publisher.

Bishop Museum Native Hawaiian Culture and Arts Program
This project is funded under the Native Hawaiian Culture and Arts Program. The views and conclusions contained in this document are those of the authors and should not be interpreted as representing the opinions or policies of the U.S. Government. Mention of trade names or commercial products does not consitute their endorsement by the U.S. Government.

Bishop Museum Press
1525 Bernice Street
Honolulu, Hawaiʻi 96817
www.bishopmuseum.org/press

ISBN: 1-58178-043-5

Cover: Postcard of Waikīkī surfers, ca. 1930. (Original photo: Frank Warren; this hand tinted postcard published by Sunny Scenes, Florida)

Page 1: A young woman and a happy surfboard invite you to the islands in this Hawaii Visitors Bureau publicity photo from about 1960.

Pages 2–3: Waikīkī surfers, ca. 1920. *(Ray Jerome Baker)*

Facing page: Commercial souvenir photo, ca. 1935.

Design by Angela Wu-Ki

Printed in Korea

Library of Congress Cataloging-in-Publication Data

Brown, DeSoto, 1954-
  Surfing : historic photographs from Bishop Museum Archives / [text] by DeSoto Brown.
      p. cm.
  ISBN 1-58178-043-5 (pbk. : alk. paper)
  1. Surfing—Hawaii—Pictorial works. 2. Surfers—Pictorial works. 3. Surfer photography. I. Bernice Pauahi Bishop Museum Archives. II. Title.

GV840.S82H383 2006
797.3'209794—dc22

2006009951

VARIOUS STYLES OF HAWAIIAN SURF RIDING

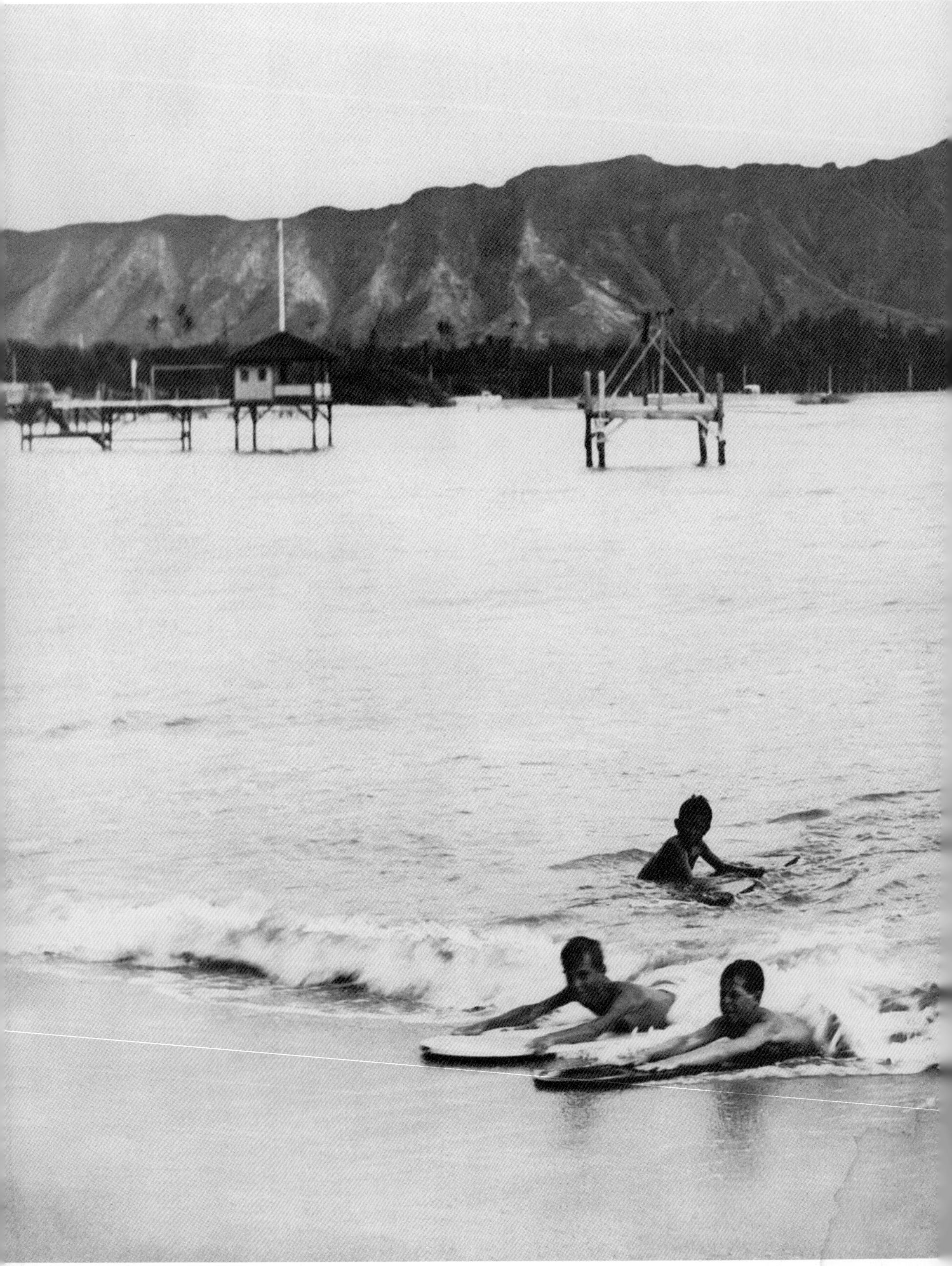

Waikīkī becomes urbanized and kiddie surfboards evolve from wood to styrofoam, but fun on the beach doesn't change from 1900 *(left)* to sixty-five years later *(above)*. *(Left: Frank Davey; above: Laurence Hata Collection)*

Dr. William T. Brigham, the first director of the Bernice Pauahi Bishop Museum (from 1896 to 1918), is flanked by two employees at the Museum's main entrance in the early years of the 20th century. Displayed behind them is a surfboard that once belonged to Chief Abner Pākī, the father of Bernice Pauahi Bishop, in whose memory the Bishop Museum was founded in 1889. By the time this photograph was taken, this treasured wooden relic was another symbol of the fast-disappearing accomplishments of traditional Hawaiian civilization. Surfing was nearly extinct.

This book is not a history of surfing, or even of surfing photography. Instead, it's a selection of historic pictures from just one collection, the Bishop Museum Archives in Honolulu, Hawai'i.

The first photographs were taken in Hawai'i in the 1840s, and Bishop Museum has been collecting photos ever since its founding forty years later. The Museum now holds over one million images of Hawai'i and the Pacific. But even with this comprehensive source to choose from, there are gaps. As it happens, this book shows mostly surfing at Waikīkī, and only within a specific time period (from the 1890s into the 1960s). This means that just a portion of surfing's full story is told. You won't see the full evolution of surfing from the time of Western contact onwards: the sport's fall and rise, its growth beyond Waikīkī and then the Hawaiian Islands, and the position it occupies in the world today. However, aspects of the more complete story fortunately are being disseminated today, and will continue to be told as research goes on. Here, instead, is a look at just part of the saga, to add information and images (some familiar and others never published before) to compliment what's already known.

Left: Freidalane Crowell gazes appreciatively at five impressive solid-wood surfboards displayed in Bishop Museum's Hawaiian Hall in 1960.

Below: One treasure of Bishop Museum is this *hale pili* (grass house), the last remaining authentic example of a once-common sight in ancient Hawai'i. It has stood for over one hundred years on the main floor of Hawaiian Hall. Propped against it is an equally authentic surfboard in this photo from about 1940.

Facing page: Kamehameha School students Clifford Kaneaiakala, Benjamin Harbottle, and Nolan Coakley dust off Chief Abner Pākī's venerable surfboard for a special Aloha Week exhibit at Bishop Museum in October 1957.

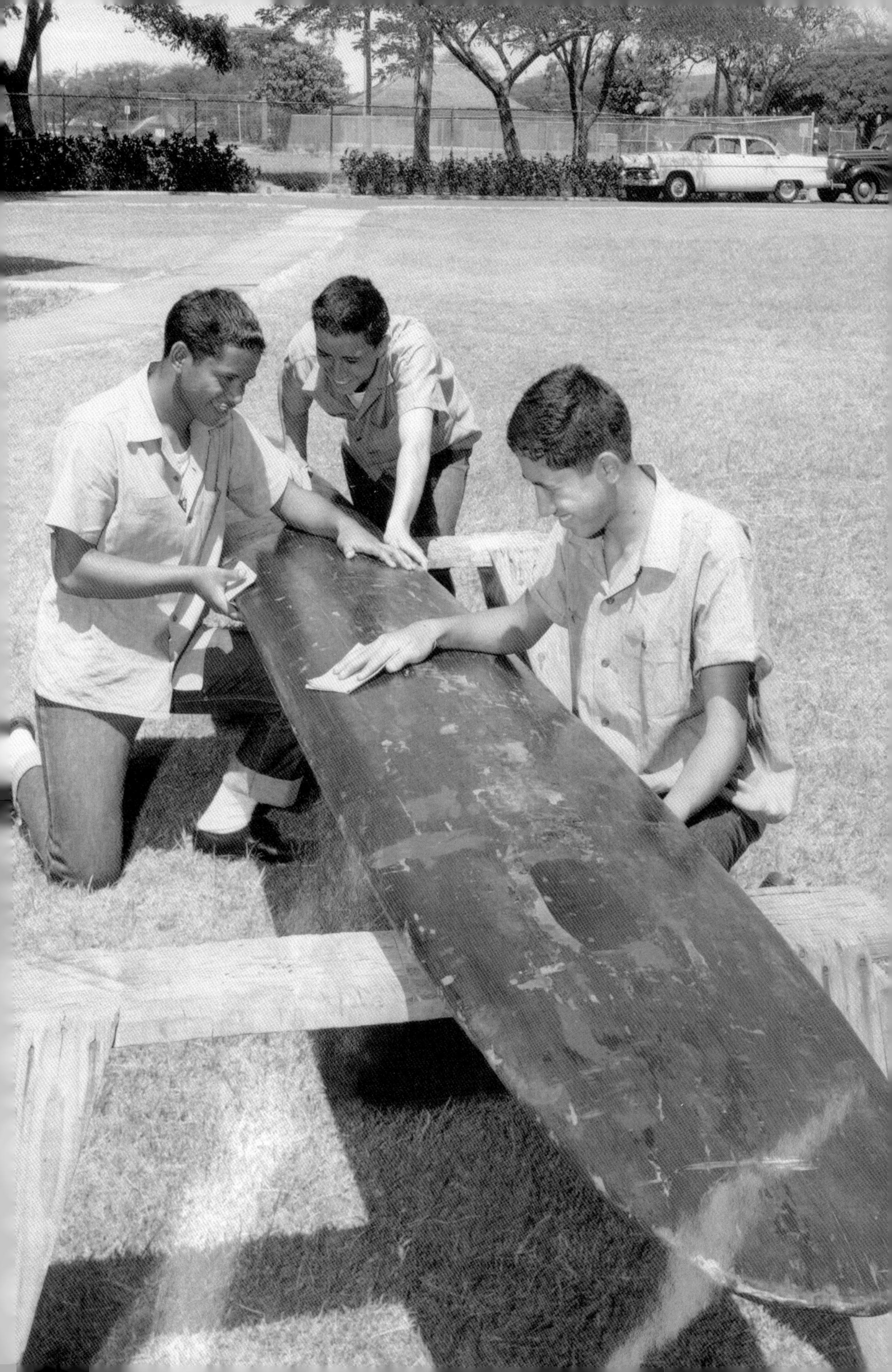

Even out of the water, the surfboard is a symbol of Hawai'i.

Above: Professional dance couple Romler and Hale pose with hula girls on the grounds of the Royal Hawaiian Hotel around 1935.

Left: The comfortable lānai of the Charles Boettcher II home in Kailua, O'ahu, displays a board with the monogram "Charly" around 1937. *(N. R. Farbman)*

Surfboards as signs.

Clockwise from top left: Elmer Lee sells souvenirs to sailors from "The Grass Hut" in Waikīkī in the middle 1930s *(N. R. Farbman)*; Duke Kahanamoku at one of the two Union Oil gas stations he managed in 1933–1934, this one at Seaside and Kalākaua Avenues in Waikīkī *(Howard Livingstone Hill)*; and appropriately-shaped signs of the Outrigger Canoe Club in Waikīkī in 1935 *(Pan-Pacific Press Bureau)* and the tiny Hāna, Maui airport in 1966 *(Robert Butterfield, Laurence Hata Collection)*.

[13

SLED OF A CHIEFESS

On the 6th of last month, N. K. Pukui, traveling agent of the Hawaiian Realty and Maturity Co., while on a tour of the Island of Hawaii, found the above illustrated sled in a cave at Hookena, Hawaii.

It is said that the oldest kamaainas of Hookena have heard from their parents and grandparents that sometime in the reign of King Keawenuiaumi, about two hundred and fifty or three hundred years ago, a high chiefess named Kaneamuna was then living at Hookena. Her principal amusement was hee holua (coasting on a sled) and hee nalu (surfing).

She had her people make a sliding ground for her on a hill just back of the little village of Hookena, and ordered a sled, or land toboggan, called a papa holua, as well as a surfing board, or a papa hee nalu. When the slide was finished she passed many pleasant hours sliding down the steep 'hill. This slide was composed of smooth stones covered with rushes. After her death her sled and surf board disappeared, and the secret of their hiding-place was never revealed.

It is believed the sled and board found in the cave belonged to the High Chiefess. They are made of the wood of the bread-fruit tree and at the present time are in very good condition. The cocoanut fiber ropes are still attached to the sled.

ANCIENT HAWAIIAN SLED FOUND IN A KONA, HAWAII, CAVE. *(Advertiser Photo.)*

Above: When surfing had nearly passed from existence, an ancient surfboard was recognized as a precious artifact. This 1905 newspaper article describes how Napoleon K. Pukui discovered a *papa hōlua* (land toboggan) and *papa he'e nalu* (surfboard), both thought to be originally of royal ownership, at Ho'okena on the island of Hawai'i. The location of these treasures is unknown today; they were never in the Bishop Museum collection.

Facing page: A Hawaiian man poses with a surfboard on an unidentified beach. Since Theodore Severin (who shot this picture) worked from 1886 to 1898, this often-reprinted image would therefore be one of the earliest known surfing pictures. But over a century later, we can't know how well this photo represents reality. As a commercial photographer, Severin (as well as those who followed him) would have wanted to produce an image that would appeal to buyers. Researchers today must remember that a photographer's original motives might not necessarily have been to document as truthfully as possible. *(Theodore Severin)*

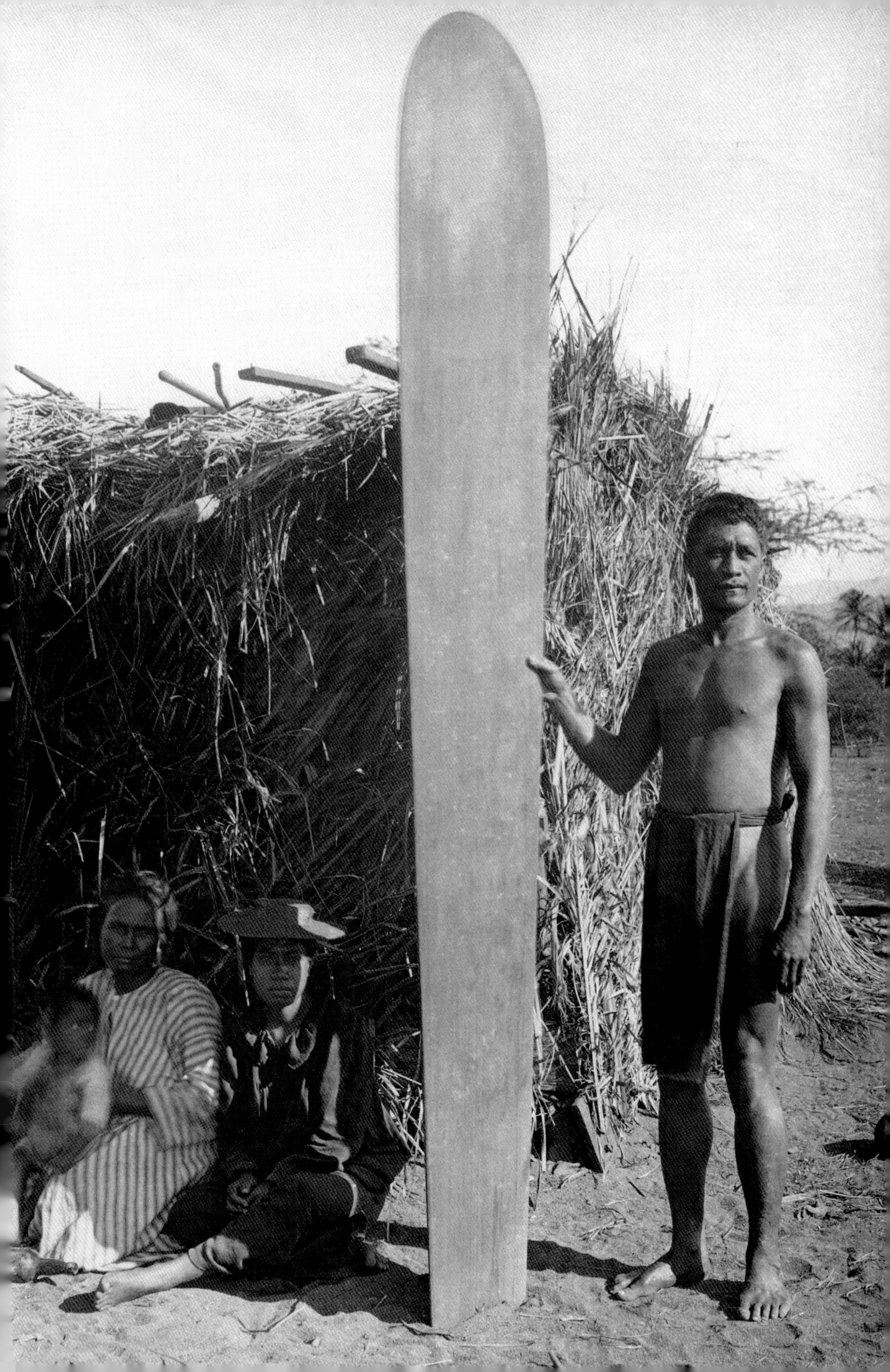

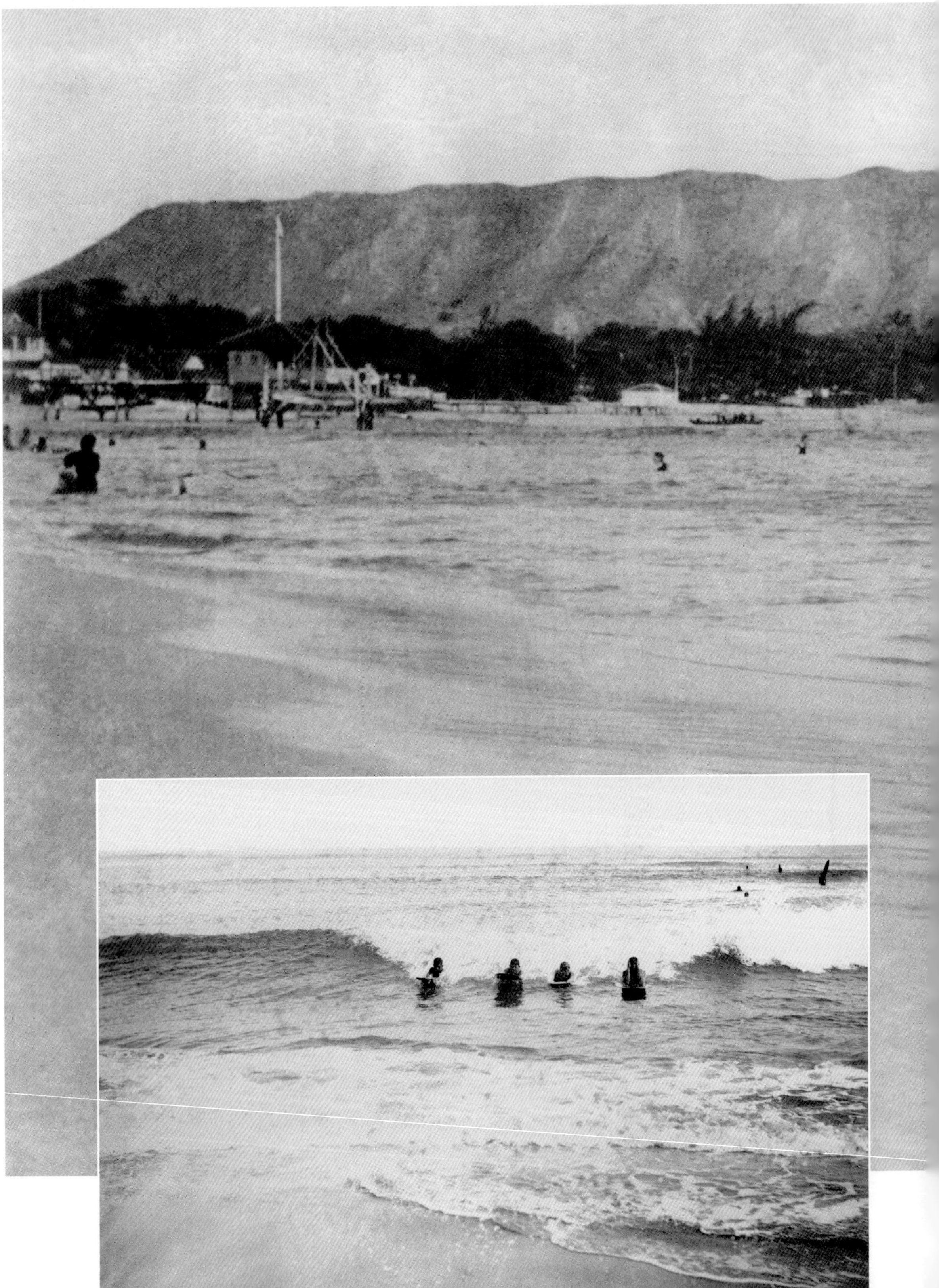

Short surfboards work well in the gentle near-shore surf of Waikīkī in two photos taken circa 1900.
(Left: Frank Davey)

10162
BOYS WITH SURF BOARDS ON BEACH AT WAIKIKI, NEAR HONOLULU, HAWAII

Surf riding has been a national sport in the Hawaiian Islands since the earliest times. Every one, old and young, male and female, joins in it. When the sea is the roughest is when they most enjoy it, and a great deal of nerve is required to steer among the rocks at the rate of forty miles an hour on the top of the highest waves. The surf board is about eight feet long by one and one-half feet wide and is made of a tough plank. The wood of the breadfruit tree is often chosen. It is slightly rounded on both sides, and kept polished with cocoanut oil until it is as smooth as glass.

The board is carried under the arm, and the surf rider swims out, diving under the incoming waves, until he gets beyond the breakers. This takes much skill, for if he does not dive at just the right time he is caught by the surf and driven back, it may be upon the rocks.

When he reaches the open sea he lies down upon the board and gets ready to ride back. The surf is made up of a number of waves, about every third one of which is larger than the rest. The smaller ones are broken before they reach the shore. He picks the largest. If by mistake he should get upon a smaller one which breaks before it reaches land or should not be able to keep his board in the proper direction on top of the swell, he would be obliged to dive and go back to the starting point to avoid the fury of the waves. On the top of the highest crest, he rides in at a fearful rate. Some of the most skilled stand up, waving their arms joyously as they coast through the breakers.

Copyright by The Keystone View Company

Stereo photos like this were popular from the late 1800s into the early 20th century. Although these two pictures at the top appear to be identical, they actually differ very slightly, having been taken by one camera with two lenses positioned a short distance apart. When mounted on a cardboard card and viewed through a handheld device, the images would appear to merge together to form one picture that looked three-dimensional. Collectors happily gathered stereo cards that showed scenes from around the world, and these were produced by the millions in a long-lasting fad. Commonly the back of the card would have explanatory text, like the one reproduced here, from about 1915.

Not only "natives" played with surfboards, for these overdressed bathers at Waikīkī are doing the same around 1911.

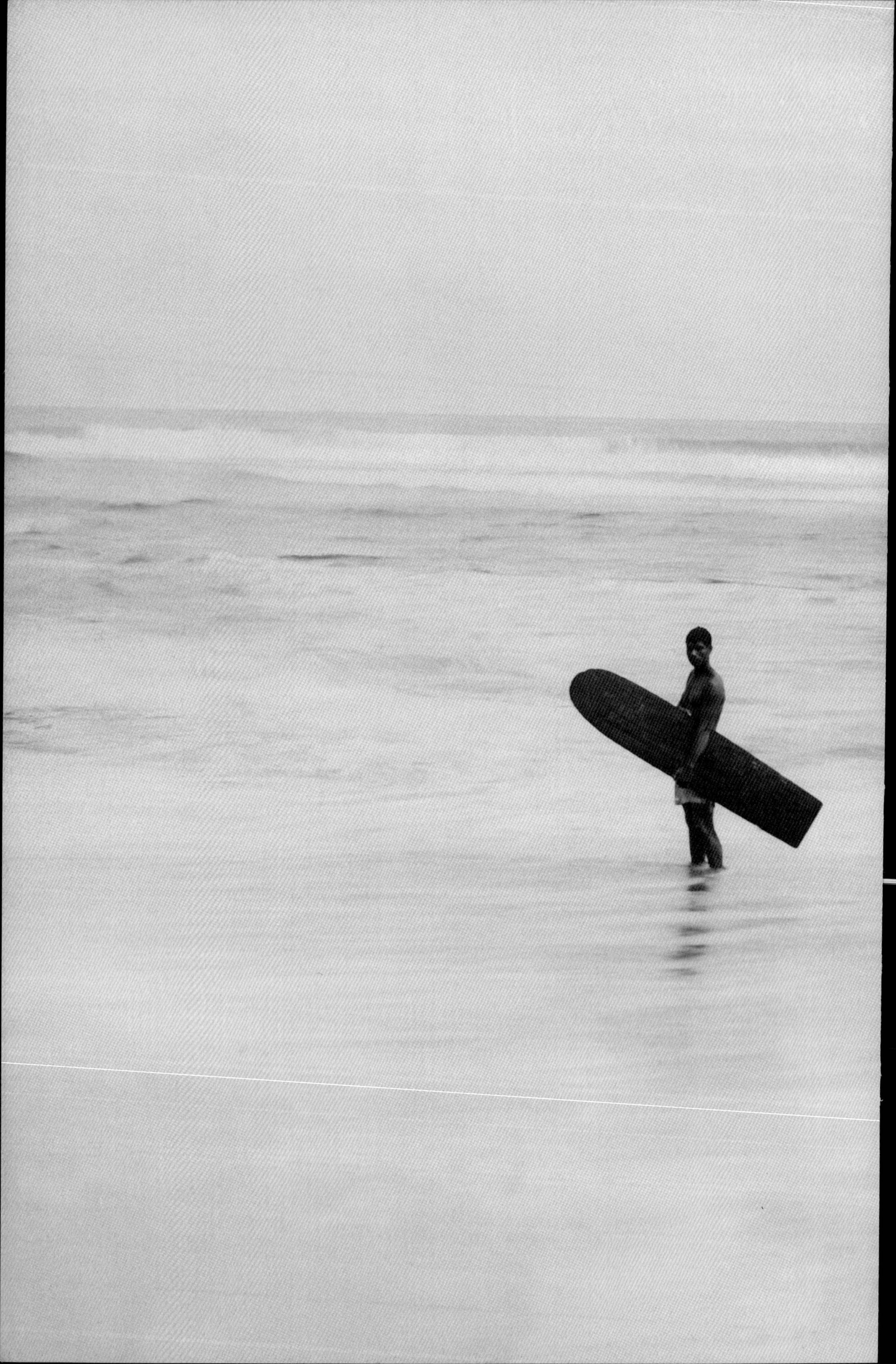

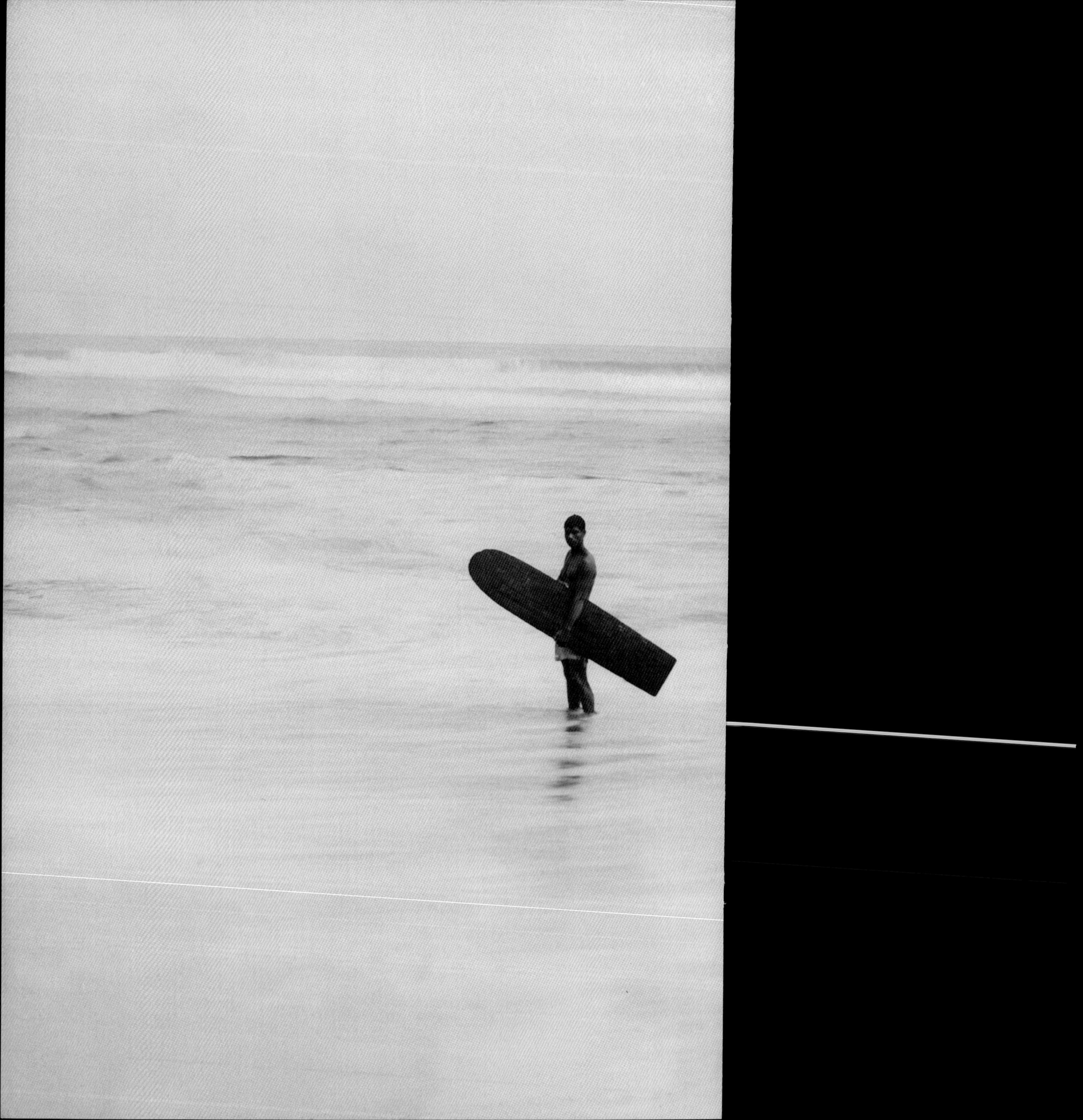

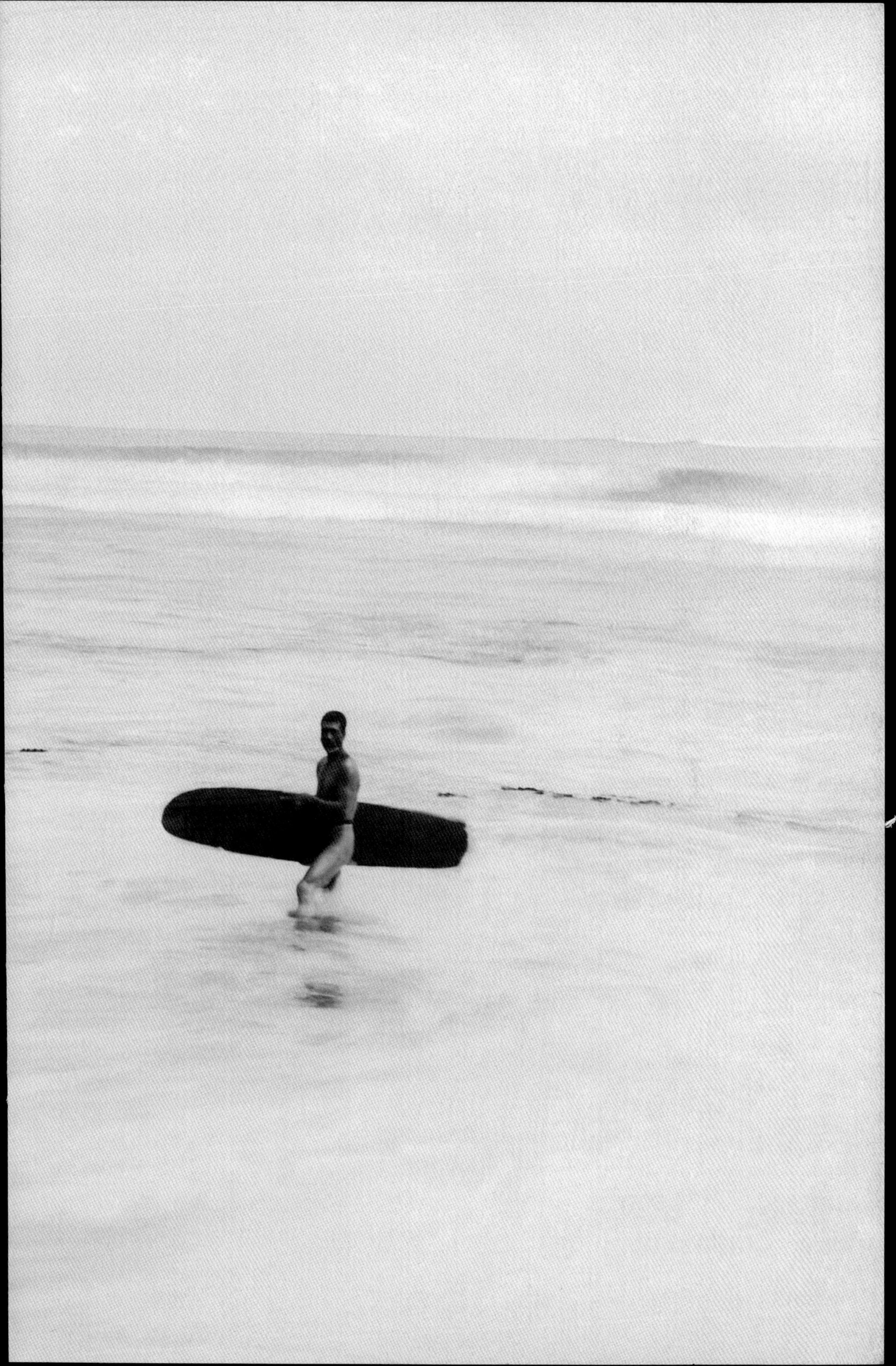

Previous pages: The location of this early photograph (most likely from the 1890s) has been identified as Hilo, probably based on a postcard from a series published by the Hilo Drug Co. and available from at least 1907 to 1913. But that cannot be correct since that bay had a black sand beach, not white, as shown here. Waikīkī is the more plausible site.

Hawai'i surfing photos taken outside of Waikīkī are uncommon before the 1950s, which makes these significant.

Facing page: This location, seen around 1910, is unidentified. Although it resembles Waimea Bay on O'ahu, the Big Island seems more likely. *(Alonzo Gartley)*

Below: Although these men certainly weren't surfing for real in these rocky shallows, this postcard shows that the sport did take place in Hilo Bay. (An inter-island steamship can be seen in the distance just above the three men; it's in the vicinity of the city's docks.) This card, a black & white image which was hand-tinted in Japan, was published around 1910.

These four pictures look similar enough that most viewers would assume they were taken together at one time. But while they all show the same man in nearly the same place, only the three images on the facing page were shot that way. They're the work of Frank Davey, who ran his business in Honolulu from 1897 to 1901. In contrast, the photographer of the picture on this page is unknown. And notice the differences: the location (judging by the buildings in the distance), the surfboard, and even the *malo* that the man is wearing and the length of his beard. This photo above is the best known of this group as it has been reprinted most frequently. *(Facing page: Frank Davey)*

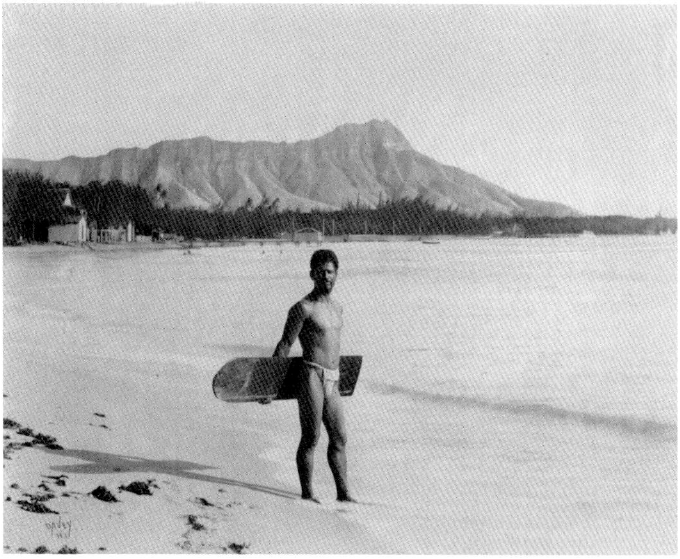

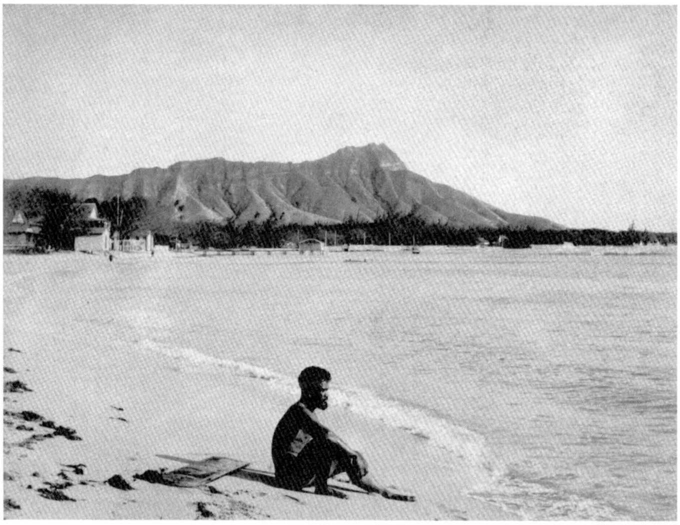

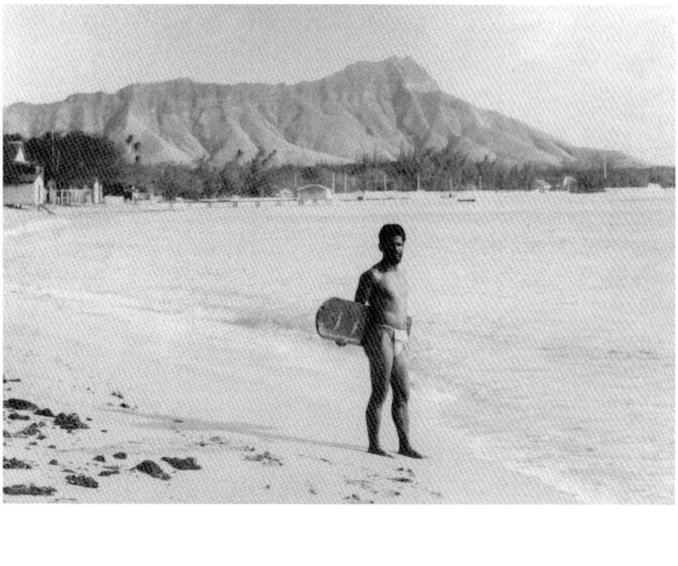

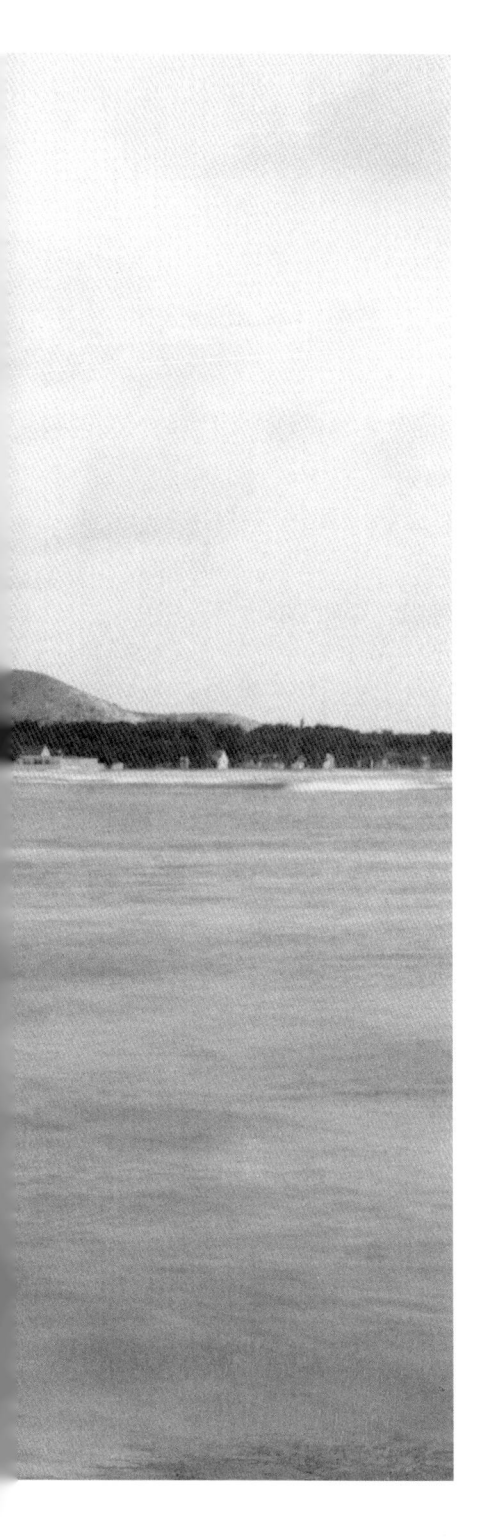

Above: These canoes are pulled up on the sand of what is now known as Kūhiō Beach in Waikīkī. They are evidence of a Hawaiian community still living in this district in 1886, whose members utilized them for sustenance fishing. While canoes would remain at Waikīkī in the years to come, their use would change significantly. *(Alfred Mitchell)*

Facing page: In the late 19th century, Hawaiian canoes at Waikīkī were gradually losing their former importance for transportation and fishing. In the coming years they would instead find roles for sport, in racing, and more notably for surfing on the dependable and usually tame waves of this famous location. Two views of this recreational use: A crew of two *haole* and two Hawaiian men photographed on January 27, 1897 *(above)*, and "Surf Boat Riding" (as photographer Frank Davey's original caption called it) from about 1900 *(below)*. Note the Hawaiian man on the right in the top picture; he is also in the four photos on pages 24 and 25. *(Below: Frank Davey)*

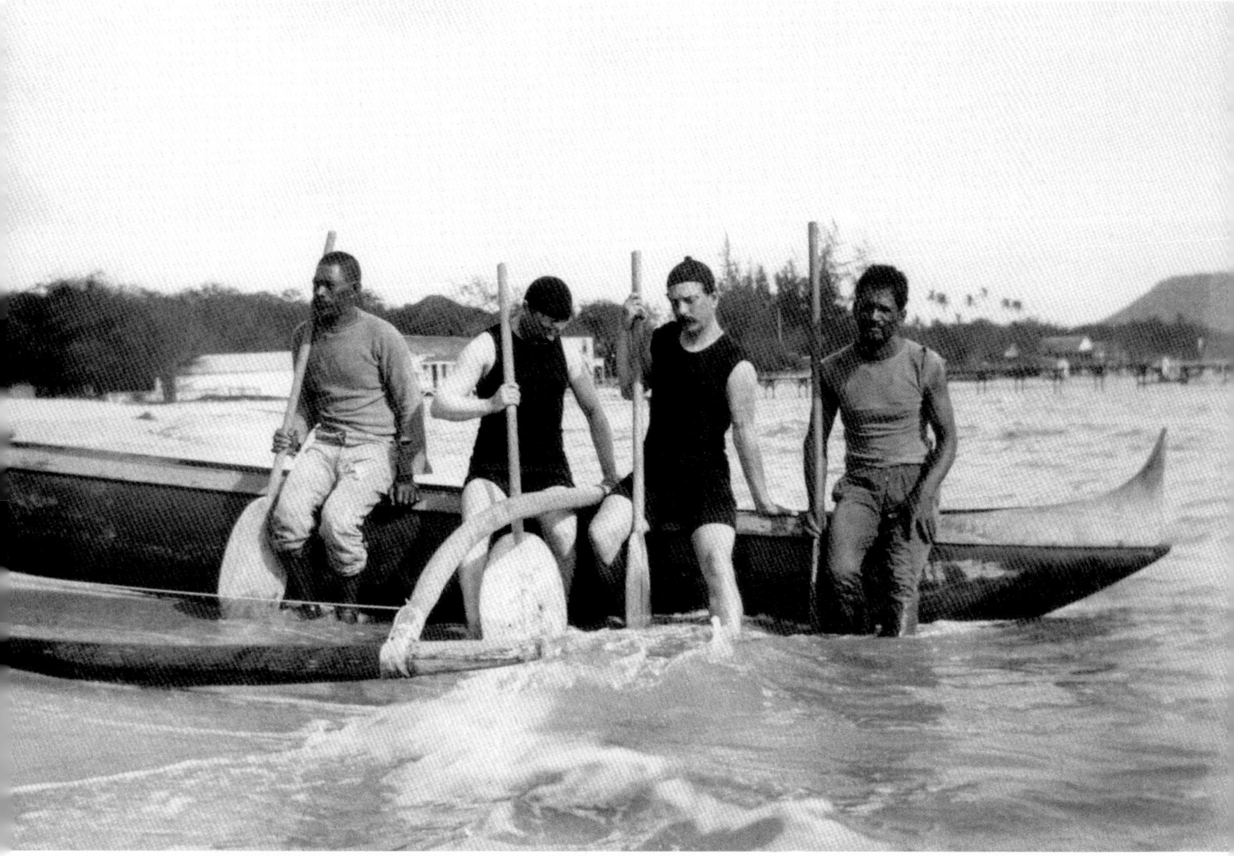

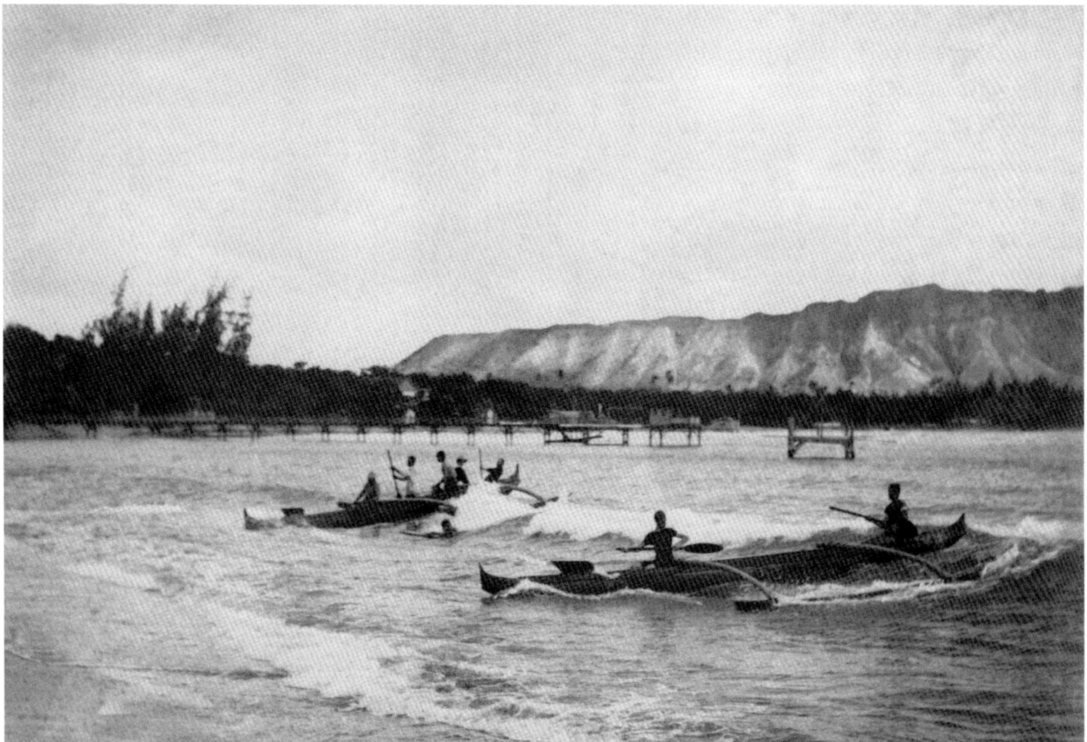

Above: Waikīkī was abruptly changed in 1901 when the Moana Hotel opened. Extending out into the ocean in front of the hotel was the Moana Pier, which in this 1907 photograph is lined with people. They, like the crowd on the beach, seem hesitant to actually enter the water.

Facing page & right: The Moana Pier, with a roofed pavilion at the end, was a wonderful place to watch surfers passing by on the small inshore waves. Both still photographers and moviemakers captured numerous images of this activity, with the surfers themselves often intentionally posing or clowning when they knew they were being filmed. The photo on the facing page shows this overall scene in 1922. At right is a postcard, one of many similar pictures that demonstrate the slightly elevated view that the pier afforded. This vantage point was lost when the deteriorated structure was demolished in 1930.

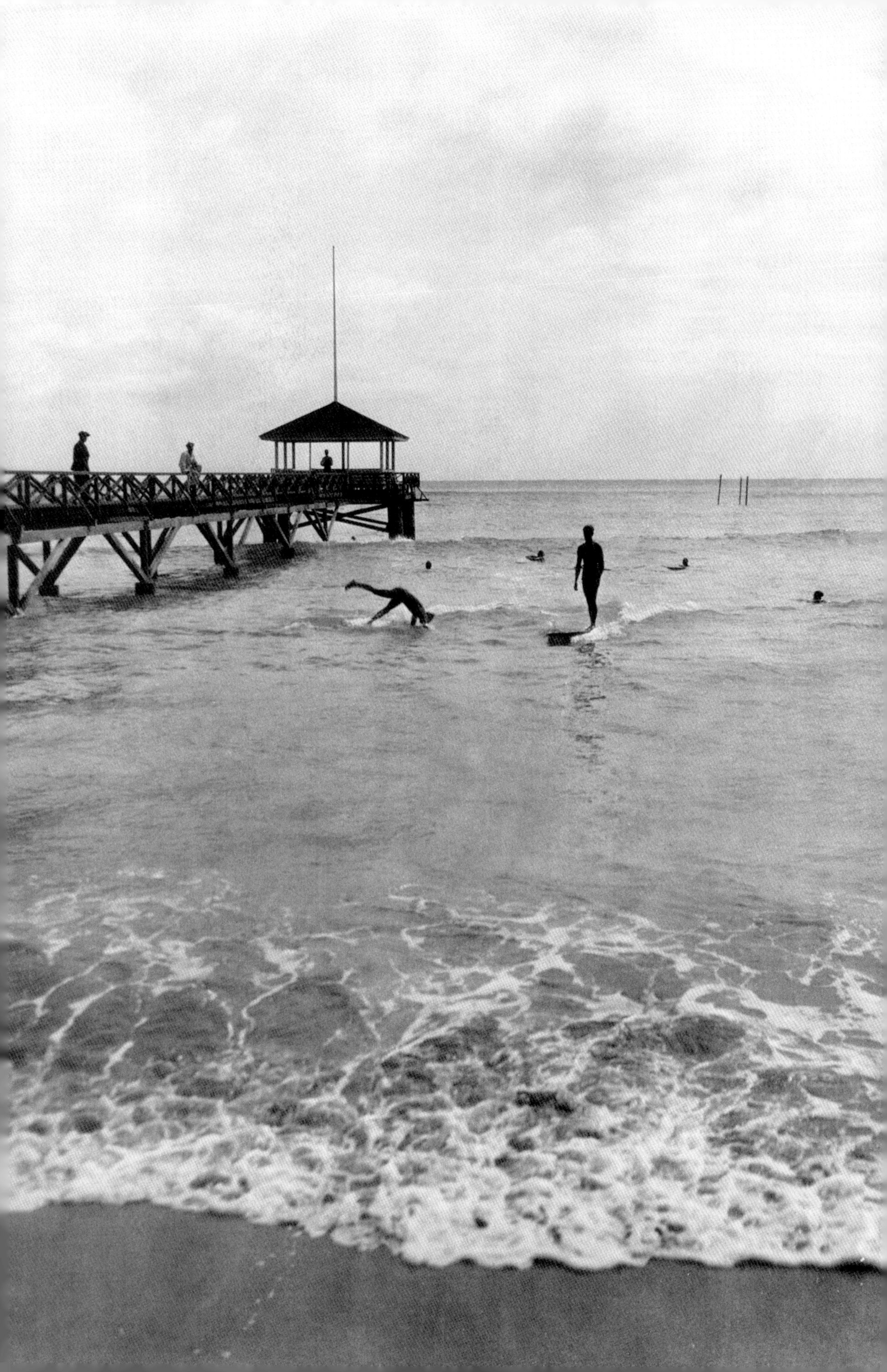

151 Surf Board Rider. Hawaiian Islands

Sport in the Surf, Honolulu, T. H.

Picture postcards were first sold in 1898, and many Hawaiian scenes proved to be perfect as postcard subjects. Surfing, of course, ranked high. On this page are two cards from the Island Curio Co., and it's appropriate that the company's founder, James Steiner, was known for his landmark home directly on Waikīkī Beach. (It's partly visible on page 64.) The top card was originally published between 1907 and 1914; the one below was on sale in the 1920s.

Facing page: This postcard was published by the Wall, Nichols Co. (a Honolulu drugstore) in about 1910. The ocean has either been considerably retouched to emphasize its roughness, or this might very well be a completely different photo combined with the view of Diamond Head. Dramatic as it is, it's not reality.

30]

Surfing at Waikiki, Honolulu.

Photo only Copyrighted.

Surf Board Riding, Hawaii.

Surf Riding at Waikiki, Honolulu.

The Hawaii & South Seas Curio Co. printed these postcards, which date from about 1910. For a faraway recipient who might not understand, the caption on the back of the card on this page explains what the pictures show: "The most popular of Hawaiian pastimes is surf swimming or heenalu. In this sport the swimmers use a light board made of koa or wiliwili. With these they swim out to sea, diving under the rollers which they meet, until they reach the outer line of breakers; then, lying flat on their boards, they balance themselves upon the forward slope of the highest breaker, and ride with the speed of a race horse toward the shore. Surfboard swimming may be seen at Waikiki near Honolulu."

Above: Christian J. Hedemann, an accomplished amateur photographer, took this picture of his son Edmund bodysurfing near Lā'ie, O'ahu, between 1905 and 1910. The Hedemanns were visiting the country home of their friends, the James B. Castles, at the time. The families had earlier been neighbors at Waikīkī, where the children of both clans learned to enjoy the ocean. James Castle's son Harold was an early participant in surfing's revival there, and married Christian Hedemann's daughter Alice in the same period. Sadly, Edmund would die prematurely in the worldwide flu epidemic in 1919. *(C. J. Hedemann)*

Right: A surfer demonstrates paddling on a full-sized wooden longboard around 1910. The angle of the view suggests this was shot from the Moana Hotel pier (see pages 28 and 29). *(Ray Jerome Baker)*

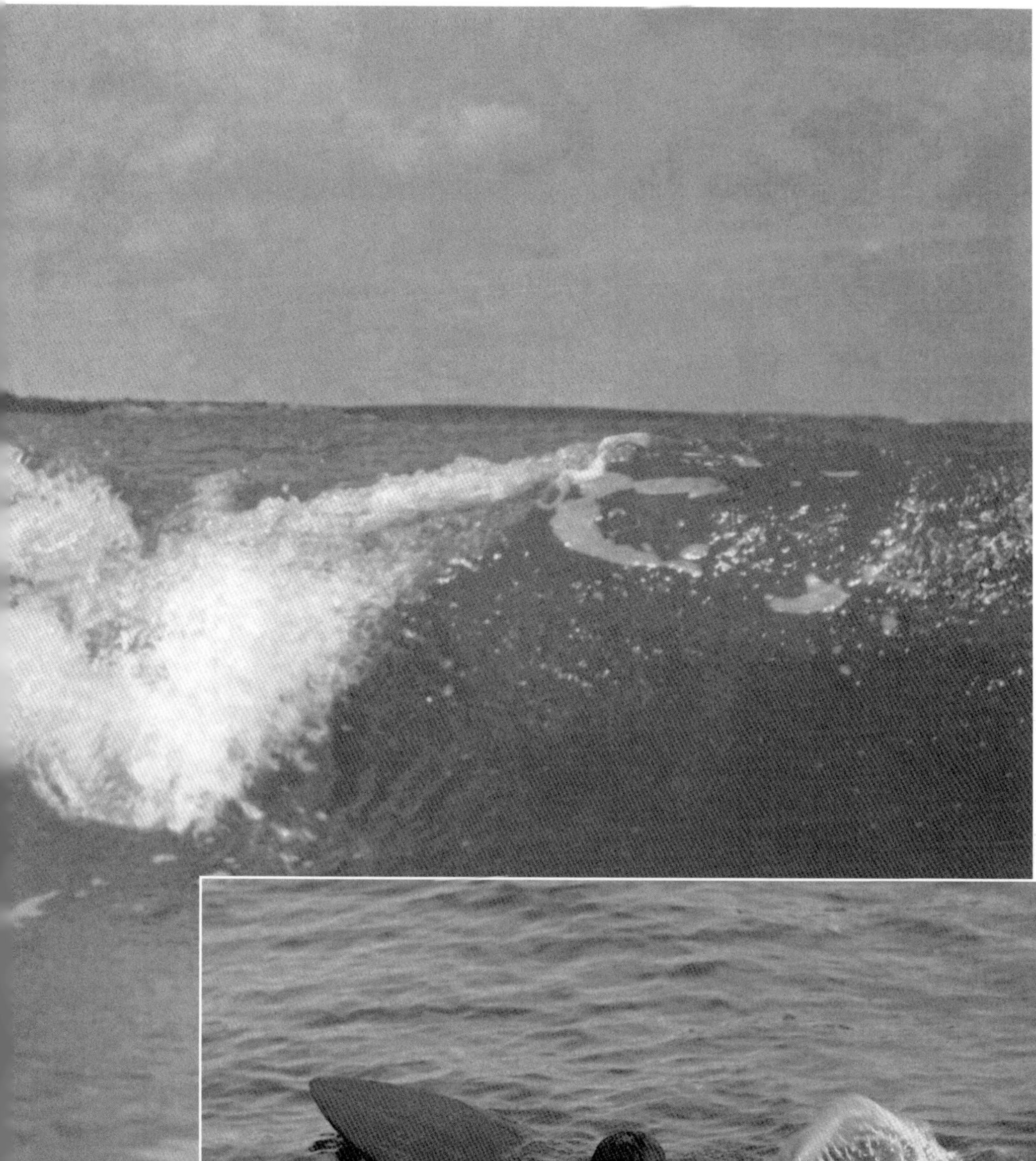

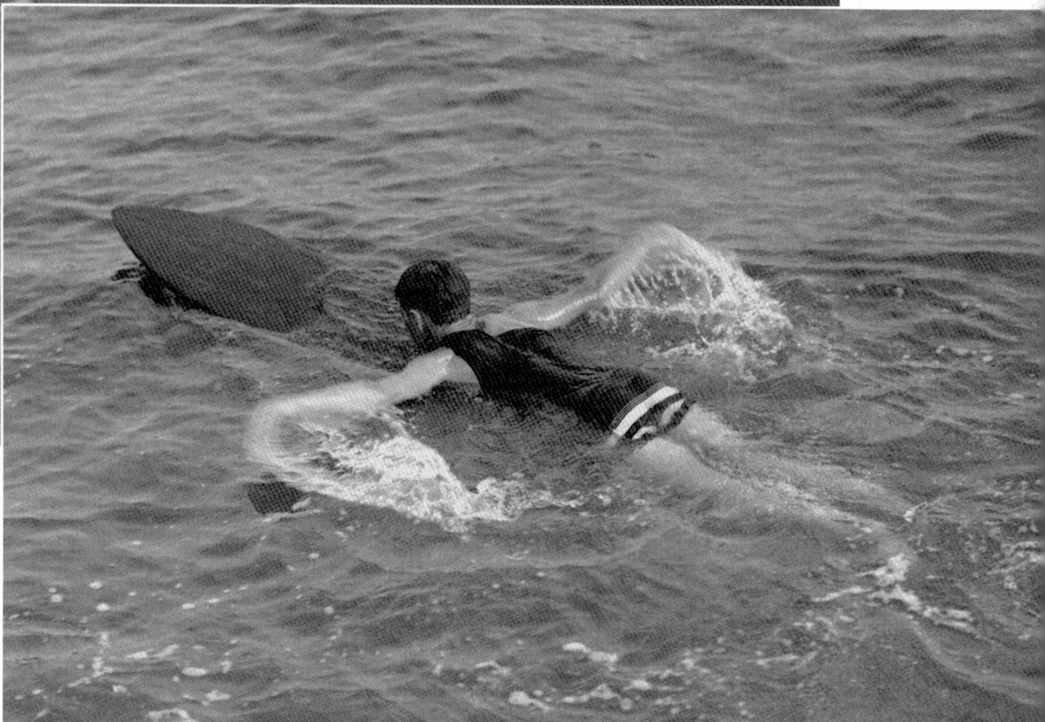

Above: This image is known to have been copied by commercial artists at least twice: for the cover of *Sunset* magazine's August 1916 issue, and for the advertising poster of the yearly Mid-Pacific Carnival held in February 1917. There is no way to know if photographer Roscoe Perkins was paid for these re-uses of his then-copyrighted photo. *(R. W. Perkins)*

Above & left: Professional photographer Ray Jerome Baker first visited Hawai'i in 1908, and settled permanently in 1910. While he desired to document Hawaiian people and their culture, he also needed to make a living from the photographs he sold, so he was always mindful of what potential buyers might find attractive. Surfing certainly qualified as a saleable subject, and it was fairly convenient for Baker to take such pictures since he lived nearby in Waikīkī. These are two of Baker's many surfing photographs, for which he unfortunately saved little or no specific information. Most likely they date from a period between 1915 and 1925.
(Ray Jerome Baker)

Above: Around 1910, a horse-drawn float moves between onlookers lining King Street at Richards Street, with the 'Iolani Palace grounds on the right. This elaborate creation is an entry in one of Honolulu's annual Floral Parades which took place around February 22, in the years from 1906 to 1917. Look closely to see that the float cleverly depicts a breaking wave propelling a small outrigger canoe with a surfboard on either side, each one carrying a boy.

Facing page: A. R. Gurrey, Jr., a pioneering surf photographer, first printed this appropriate quote in his small art photo book, *The Surf Riders of Hawaii*, around 1910. It was republished in *The Mid-Pacific Magazine* (again coupled with one of Gurrey's surfing photos) in the August 1911 issue. In turn, Ray Jerome Baker used it for his own version perhaps a few years later, which is shown here. The text is the third to last stanza of the epic poem "Childe Harold's Pilgrimage" by the influential English poet Lord Byron, originally published between 1812 and 1818. In four lengthy cantos, the title character describes his lifetime travels, poignantly anticipating his approaching death as the poem ends. A well-educated reader of the early 20th century would have no doubt recognized the source of these words.
(Ray Jerome Baker)

And I loved thee, Ocean; and my joy
   Of youthful sports was on thy breast to be
Borne, like thy bubbles, onward: from a boy
   I wantoned with thy breakers,—they to me
Were a delight; and if the freshening sea
   Made them a terror, 'twas a pleasing fear:
For I was as it were a child of thee,
   And trusted to thy billows far and near,
And laid my head upon thy mane,—
   As I do here.
                Lord Byron

Perky young Gertrude McQueen shows off fashionable beachwear on Waikīkī between 1915 and 1920, including lace-up boots. Considering the weight of the surfboard she's seated on, she probably was not able to make much use of it—or even lift it. *(Ray Jerome Baker)*

Long-haired Maxie Mitchell poses by herself, and with fellow members of the traveling Jack Mcgee vaudeville troupe, in the fall of 1914 at Waikīkī. The picture on the left was printed on the cover of the sheet music for the song "My Waikiki Mermaid" that probably dates from 1915 or 1916. (Another version of the photograph contains a partial view of Diamond Head on the left.) Judging by the condition of her hair, Maxie has not actually immersed herself in the water despite her familiarity with surfboards. *(Ray Jerome Baker)*

[41]

Right: On March 23, 1911, this happy group posed with a small outrigger canoe. *(L. E. Edgeworth)*

This page, above: A six-man canoe floats just offshore, with the beach pavilion of the Seaside Hotel visible at far right. **Below:** A group of *haole* men whoop it up on a brisk ride shoreward. By this time, canoes at Waikiki had transitioned to recreational use.
(Ray Jerome Baker)

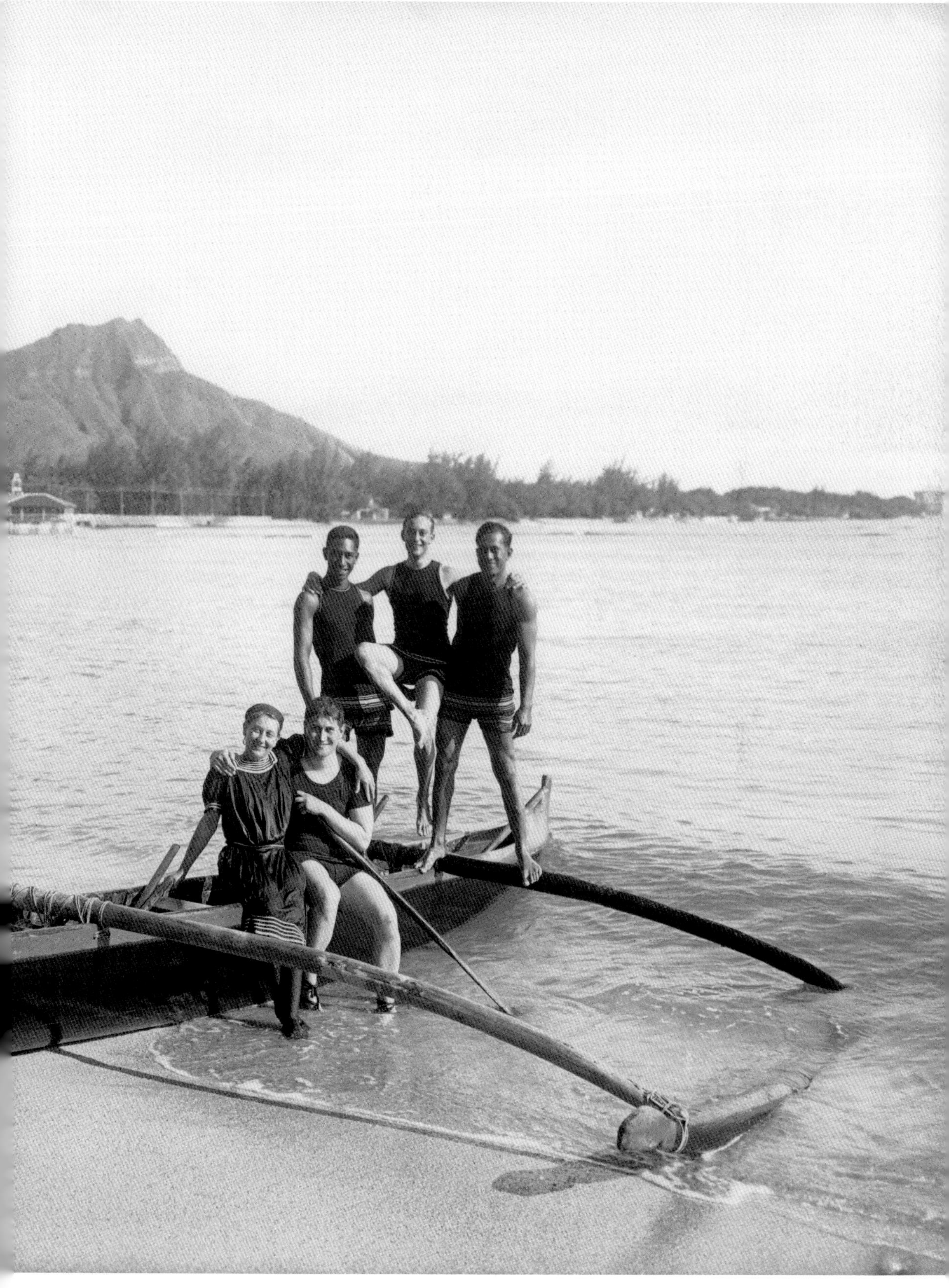

5th Group (Obs.) Moana Hotel B-613, 562-44, 9-9-20, 2:30 P.M. 1500.

Left: This is one of the earliest aerial views of Waikīkī, shot by a U.S. Army plane on Sept. 9, 1920. The Moana Hotel and its pier are in the center, with the Outrigger Canoe Club (the prime instigator of surfing's revival) to the left, on the beach. The Ala Wai Canal has not yet been dug in this part of Waikīkī, and inland of Kalākaua Avenue much of the area is still under water and contains rice fields. 'Āpuakēhau Stream, although difficult to see, feeds the beachside lagoon between the Moana and the Outrigger. Its flow of fresh water has kept the area immediately offshore clear of coral growth. The beach itself has yet to undergo the dramatic sand replenishments which would occur regularly in the decades to come, and thus the natural wave patterns have not yet been greatly altered. *(U. S. Army)*

Above: *The Honolulu Advertiser* shot this dramatic scene in 1925. *(Honolulu Advertiser)*

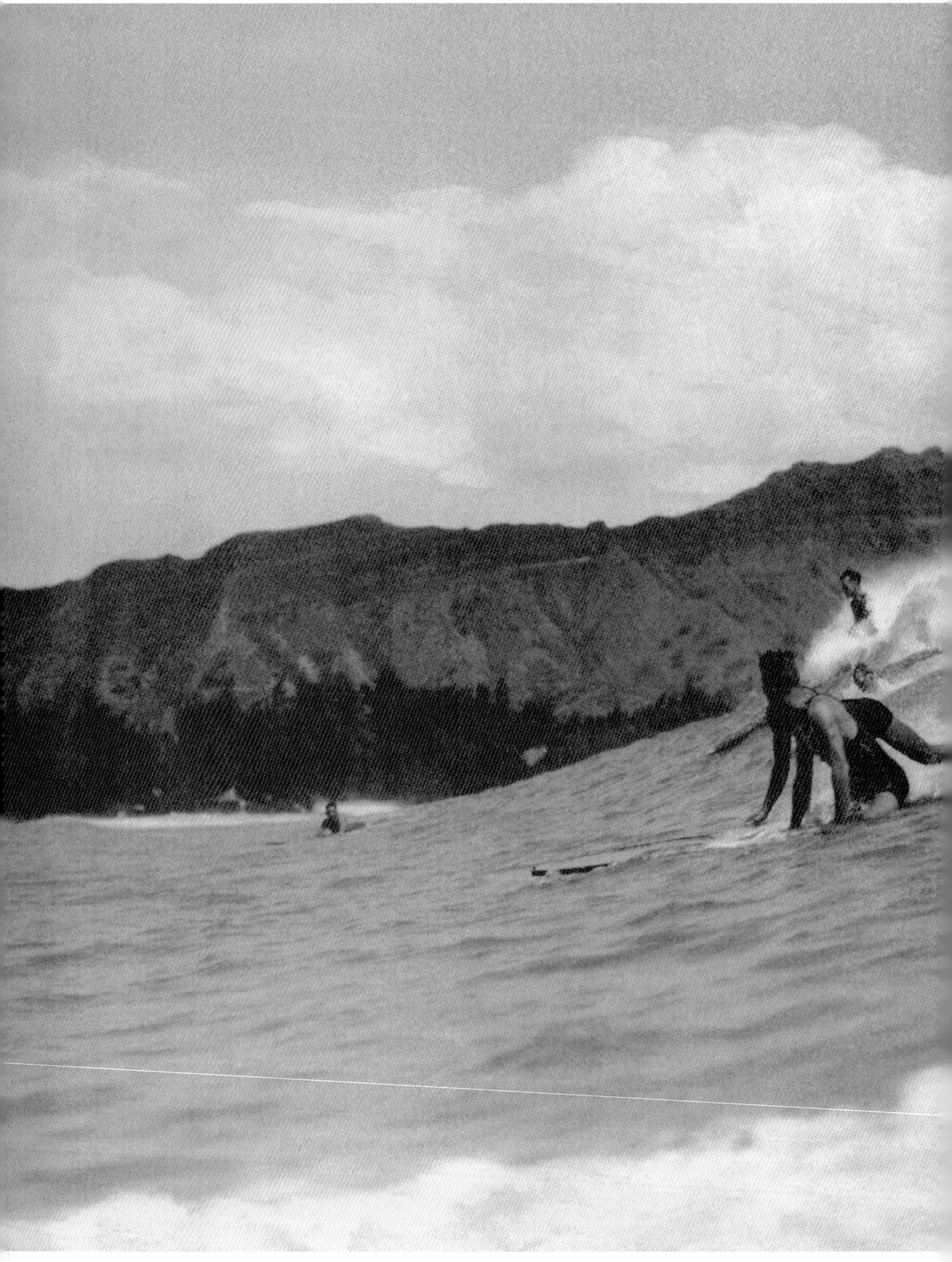

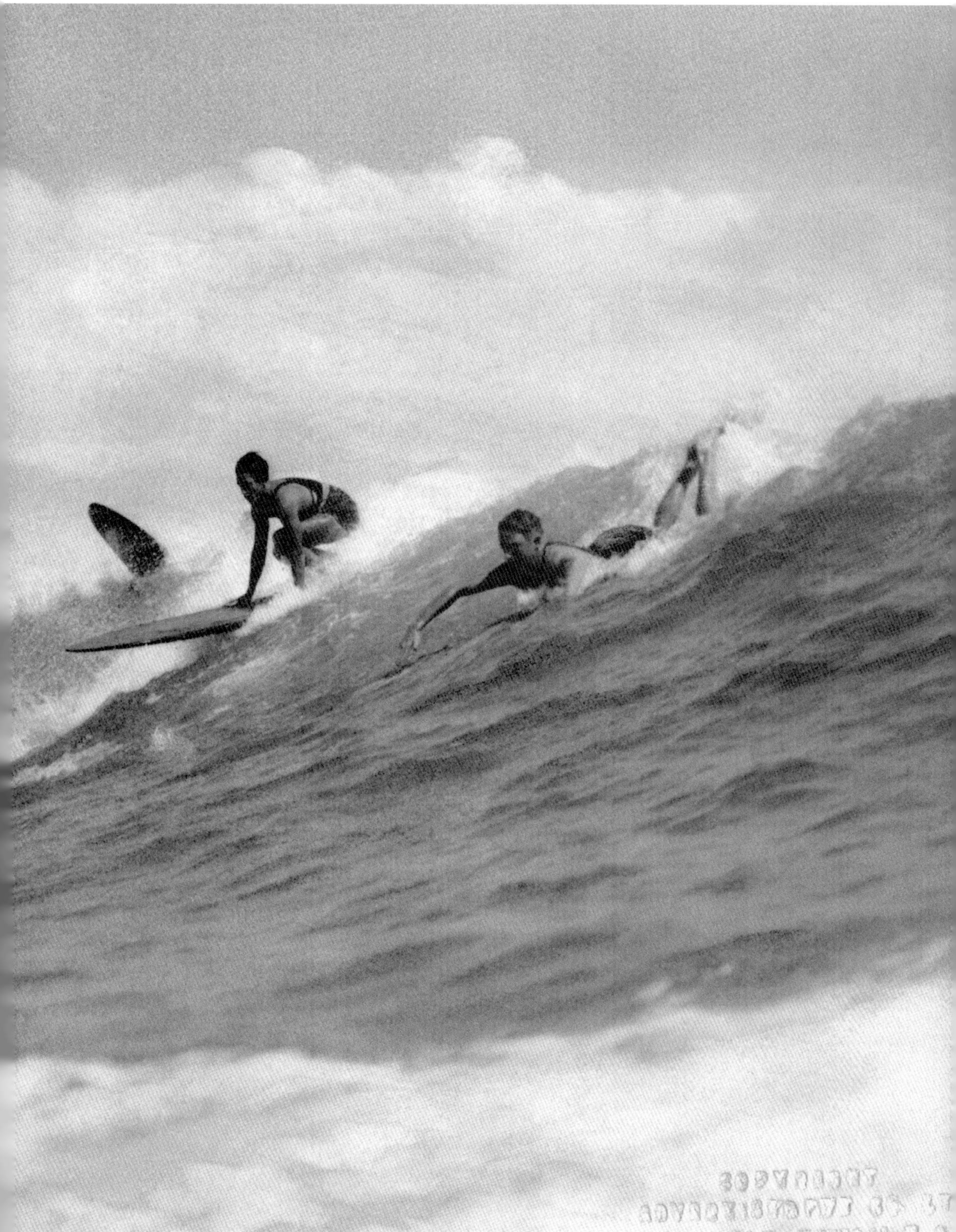

Previous pages: A dynamic and action-filled view of multiple surfers at Waikīkī, similar to the photo on pp. 44–45. Both were shot at the same time by the same photographer. *(Honolulu Advertiser)*

Above: The surfer on the left makes this process look especially easy. Although part of the Ray Jerome Baker collection, it is not certain that this circa 1920 photo was actually shot by him. *(Ray Jerome Baker Collection)*

The headstand was a favorite Waikīkī surf stunt in the years of heavy solid boards. At top is a commercially-sold souvenir photo, below is a postcard. Both probably date from between 1915 and 1920.

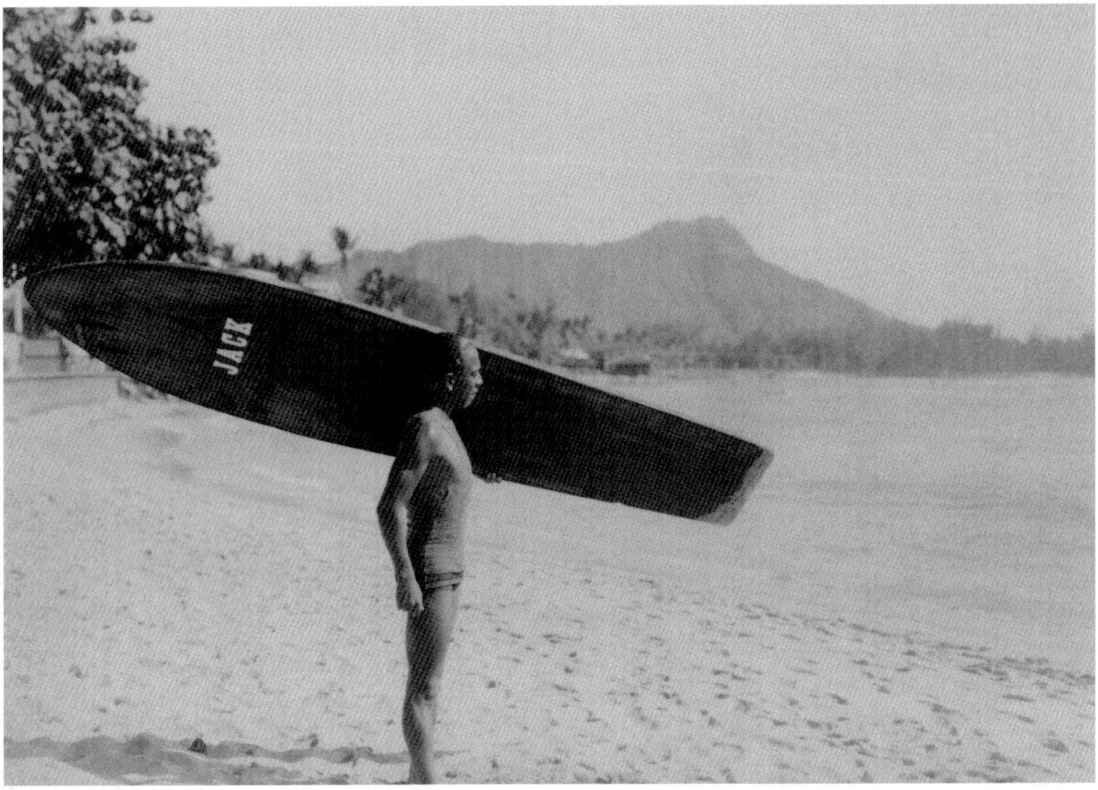
JACK

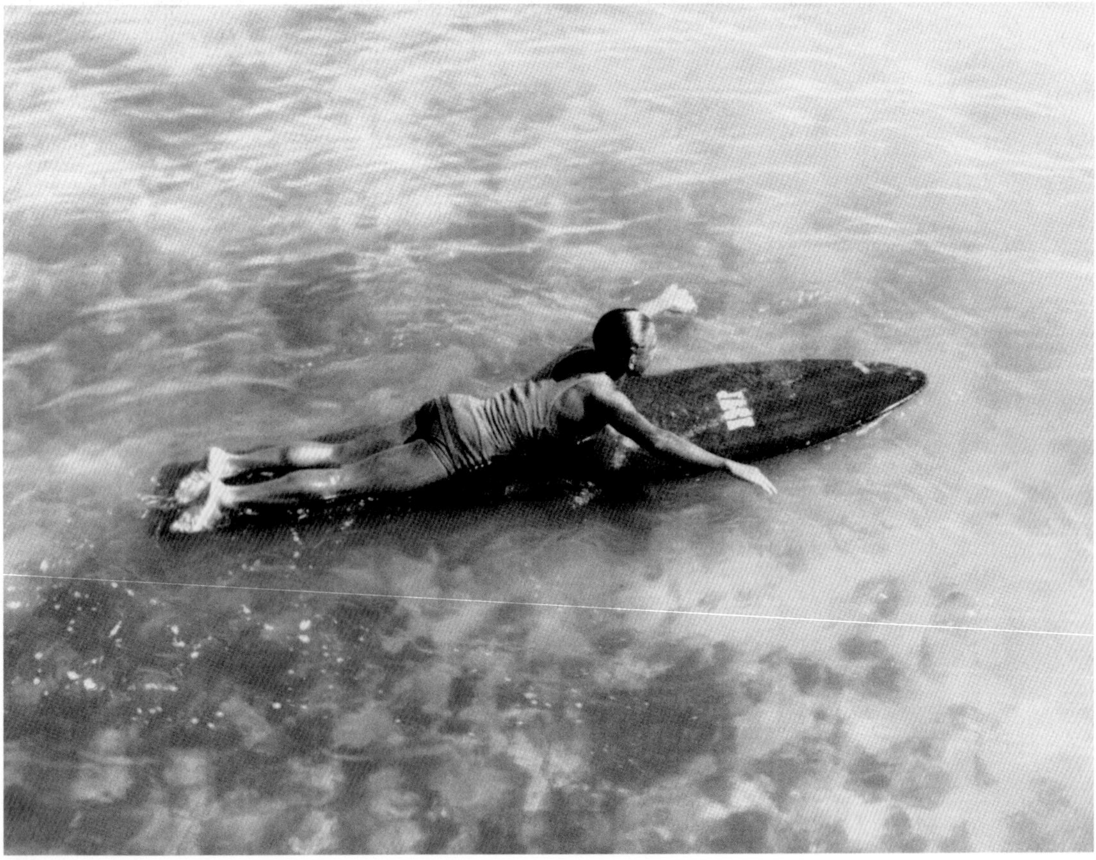

Above: Here's Hollywood movie star Betty Compson on location in Hawai'i to film *The White Flower* in 1922. In this movie, she played a *hapa haole* woman who fell in love with a pineapple company executive; when the man's fiancée joined him from the mainland, Betty got a *kahuna* to curse her rival. Fortunately, she then changed her mind and managed to have the threat rescinded. (Note that the man second from the right is not Duke Kahanamoku, even though he's posing with Duke's board.)

Facing page: Film innovator Burton Holmes was famous for his travelogues, and in 1898 he had the distinction of being the second person to actually shoot movie footage in Hawai'i. Years later, in 1926, his cameraman Franklin LaVarre took these two photos of Waikīkī beachboy Sam Colgate as part of Holmes's production entitled *Happy Hawaii*. This program, presented throughout the U.S., consisted of alternating slide and movie sequences and was narrated in person by Burton Holmes himself. The promotional description claimed grandiosely that audiences would see "The Most Thrilling Pictures Of Surf-Board And Canoe Surf-Riding Ever Taken...Filming The Experts From A Canoe On The Crest Of An Advancing Breaker." A home movie version of this same sequence, sold to the public as *Surfing - The Famous Sport of Waikiki*, can be viewed in the Bishop Museum collection. It's a nice little film, but it doesn't live up to the hype quoted above. *(Franklin LaVarre)*

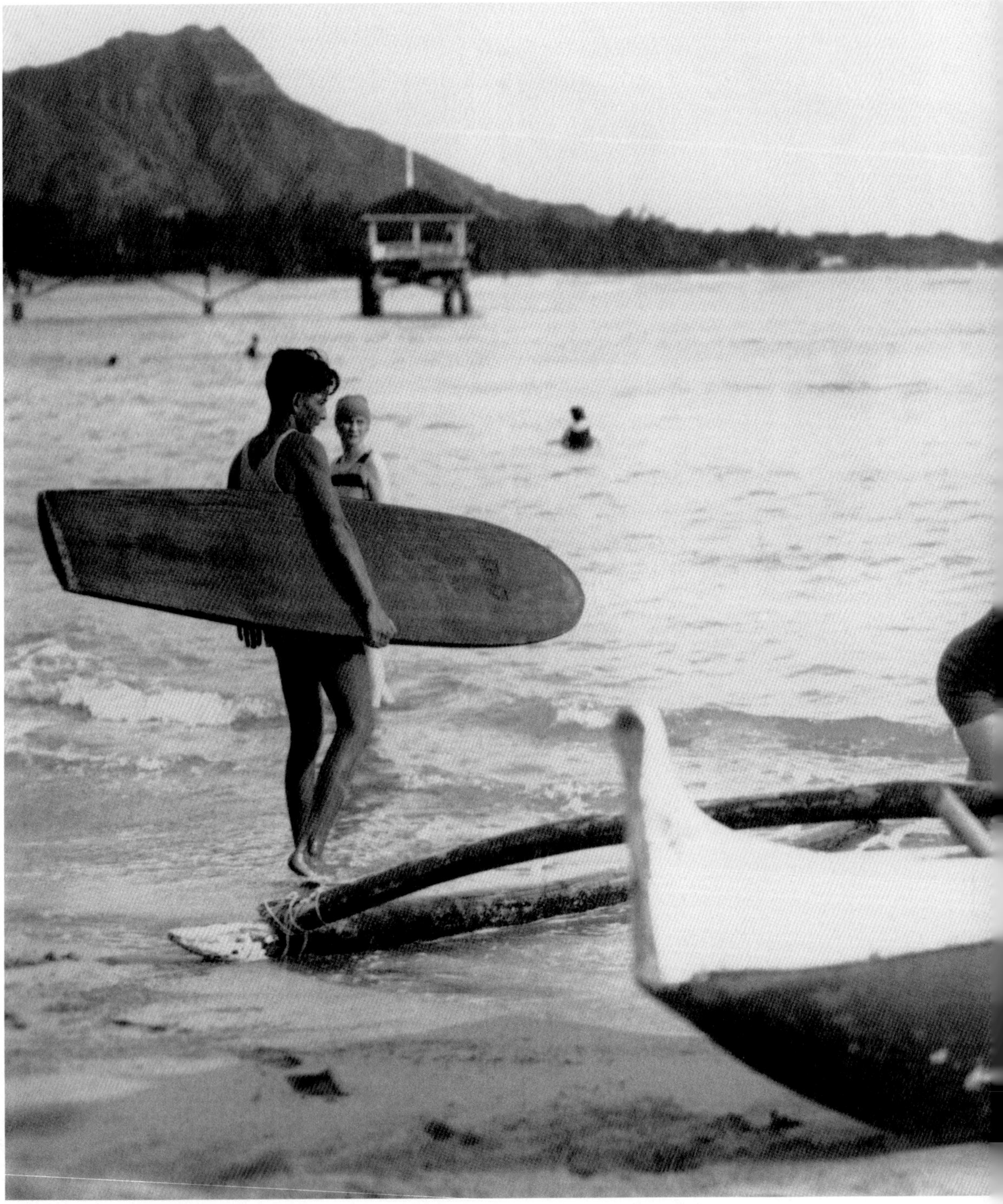

Left: The unassuming man leaning on the canoe in this 1927 photo is George Armitage, a prime mover and tireless promoter in the Hawaii Tourist Bureau. When the Bureau closed early in World War II (with pleasure travel being prohibited), Armitage and his wife started their own company to publish postcards and souvenir booklets for military personnel. It's appropriate that he should have experienced Waikīkī water sports in person in order to sell the fun to others.

Below: Seattle visitors Mr. and Mrs. H. W. Bryan (right) ready themselves for a canoe ride at Waikīkī in 1925. Visible at the far right of this photo is the start of the construction of the Royal Hawaiian Hotel. Its opening two years later would be another significant step in Waikīkī's growth, which would include the sponsoring of an official beachboy organization (the Waikiki Beach Patrol) in the 1930s.

me and my surfboard at waikiki in a cove

The surfboard as everybody's favorite prop in the teens and twenties.
Clockwise from top left: Rose Heather at Gray's Beach *(Ray Jerome Baker)*, Sidney Heyser at Kālia in 1926, an unknown woman in 1925, a surfboard marked "Mokuahi / Owned By / Harry Newcomb" in 1913, Miss Train in front of the Outrigger Canoe Club about 1915 *(Ray Jerome Baker)*, Mr. and Mrs. H. W. Bryan in 1925, and Patrick Powers at Waimānalo around 1917.

[55

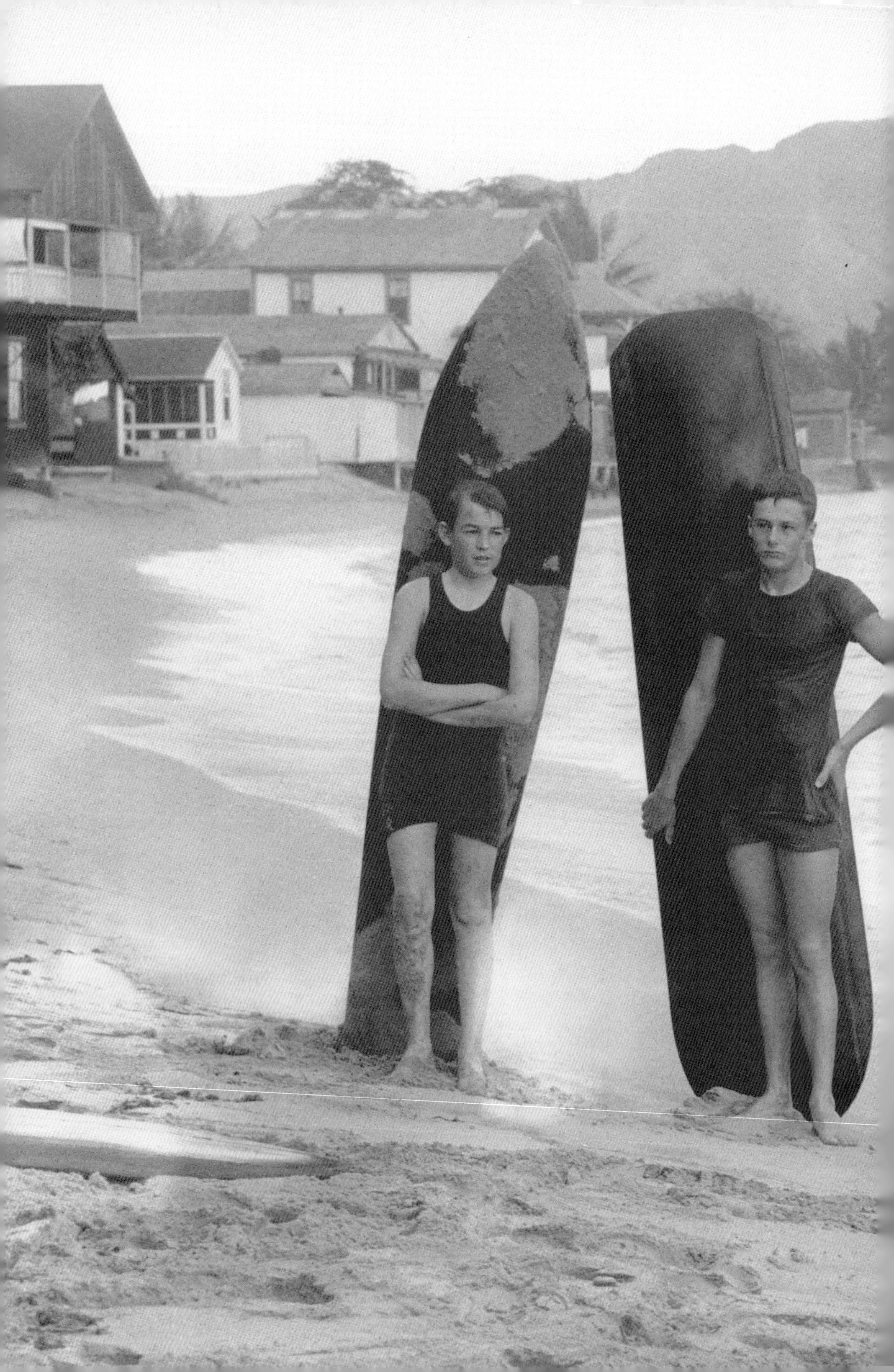

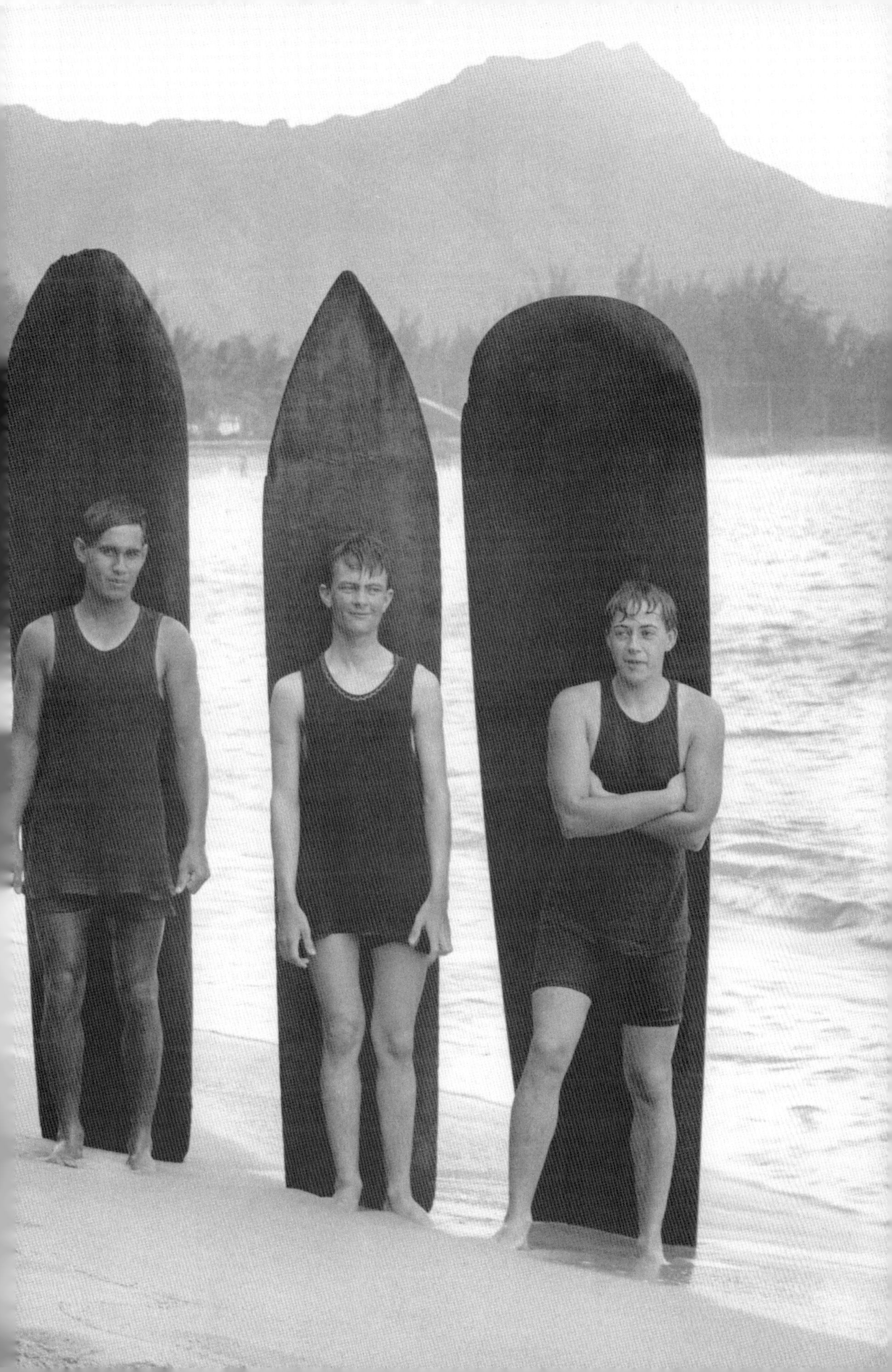

Previous pages: Five young guys and their boards around 1910. In the center is sportsman and musician Dudie Miller, who would be well known when he grew older. *(Ray Jerome Baker)*

This page, top: A Red Cross life-saving class in Waikīkī in 1920. **Middle:** The Waikiki Beach Patrol between 1935 and 1937, including second from left, Pua Kealoha (also a musician and singer); third, Sally Hale; and sixth, Tom Blake. **Bottom:** Beachboys serve as extras for the location filming of the Hollywood movie *Waikiki Wedding* in 1937. *(N. R. Farbman)*

Surfboard water polo was briefly popular, demonstrated in the ocean in front of the Royal Hawaiian Hotel in the late 1920s and early '30s. The aggressive mix of these huge boards probably made it awkward and occasionally dangerous. The caps these men are wearing suggest that they're players: Melvin Paoa, Charles Amalu, Ernest Wilson, Curly Cornwell, Malcolm Paoa, and Louis Kahanamoku. Behind them is the dining room of the Moana Hotel; this wing was demolished just after World War II.

This page: Leisurely fun in the uncrowded ocean could be had offshore of the Royal Hawaiian *(top)* and Moana Hotels *(bottom)* in the middle 1930s. *(N. R. Farbman)*

A squadron of army biplanes passes over Waikīkī in 1933. Inland of the only two large hotels, there are still good-sized tracts of undeveloped land. Offshore, the surf breaks are mostly unoccupied. *(U.S. Army)*

To
Mr & Mrs Robertson
With "Best Wishes"
Philip

To Mr & Mrs Robertson
With "Best Wishes"
Philip K Auna
1/1/29

THE HAWAII TOURIST BUREAU
Presents
THE ISLAND OF OAHU
Territory of Hawaii, U.S.A.

Produced by
Palmer Miller & Curtis F. Nagel

Narration — **Don Blanding**   Music — **Keaumoku Louis**

PASSED BY NATIONAL BOARD OF REVIEW
Copyrighted MCMXXXIV

Facing page: Philip K. Auna autographed these photos of himself and his talented pet, Night Hawk the surfing dog, for some mainland visitors in early 1929. (Around this time, the same pair appeared in a souvenir film called *On The Waves At Waikiki*, which can also be found in Bishop Museum's collection.) In the 1950s another beachboy, Joseph Kaopuiki, performed similar stunts at Waikīkī with his canine buddy Sandy; this later dog's surfing days ended in 1960 when he died at the age of twelve.

Above: The title shot of a 1934 travelogue, *The Island Of Oahu*, uses this internationally famous view of Hawai'i's unique sport. This film was one of six commissioned at the time by the Hawaii Tourist Bureau; all were made by the same Hollywood production company. They were shown in movie theaters as well as summertime fairs and expositions throughout the U.S. over the next several years, and even on cruise ships steaming to the islands. All can be viewed today at Bishop Museum Archives. As narrator Don Blanding states in *The Island of Oahu*, "There is no sport on earth more thrilling than surfriding. It was the sport of kings in the past, and every newcomer to Hawaii today is gripped by the ambition to ride one of these mighty chargers of the surf."
(Christine Takata)

Serving as steersman for this canoe off Waikīkī around 1935 is Duke Kahanamoku, and sitting just in front of him is waterman "Dad" Center. The buildings onshore include (from left) the Hustace home, the Steiner mansion (between the two women), and the Waikiki Tavern and Inn at far right. *(N. R. Farbman)*

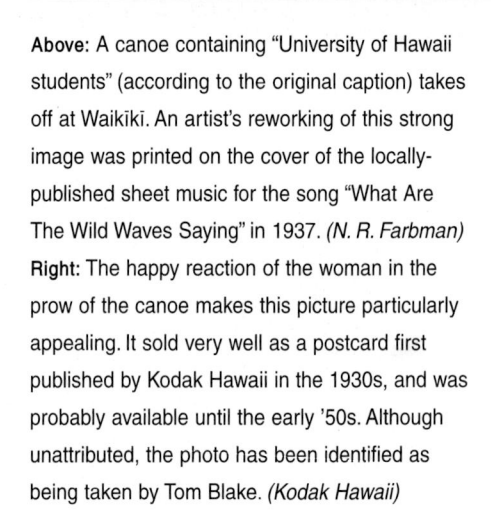

Above: A canoe containing "University of Hawaii students" (according to the original caption) takes off at Waikīkī. An artist's reworking of this strong image was printed on the cover of the locally-published sheet music for the song "What Are The Wild Waves Saying" in 1937. *(N. R. Farbman)*
Right: The happy reaction of the woman in the prow of the canoe makes this picture particularly appealing. It sold very well as a postcard first published by Kodak Hawaii in the 1930s, and was probably available until the early '50s. Although unattributed, the photo has been identified as being taken by Tom Blake. *(Kodak Hawaii)*

Surf Riding, Waikiki

[65]

Thomas Edward Blake, Jr. is a fascinating figure in the history of surfing. He was born far from the ocean in Milwaukee, Wisconsin in 1902. Seeing a brief bit of film showing surfing at Waikīkī in about 1910 made a major impression on him, as did his first personal meeting with Duke Kahanamoku at a Detroit movie theater ten years later. A disrupted childhood, along with his introspective and sensitive outlook, sent Tom Blake out into the world as a wanderer; a talent for swimming (although he didn't learn until the age of 17) and a love of nature eventually drew him to surfing. He first rode the surf in California in the early 1920s, and in 1924 visited Hawai'i. He would continue to visit the islands, and to live here for short periods, until his last trip in 1968. After an adventure-filled life, Tom ended up back in Wisconsin, where he died in 1994.

But Tom Blake was not merely an interesting character. He pushed surfing ahead not only by his personal athletic achievements, but even more through the practical design changes he created for surfboards.

Facing page: Tom Blake, at right, joins a group on Waikīkī Beach in a publicity photo in the middle 1930s. *(N. R. Farbman)*

This page, above: Tom first came to Hawai'i in 1924 and bought this surfboard (the first of many he would own) for $25. The photo was taken at Waikīkī, with the Seaside Hotel in the background. **Below:** Tom surfing at Waikīkī when he was a lifeguard and beachboy in the Waikiki Beach Patrol from 1935 to 1937. *(N. R. Farbman)*

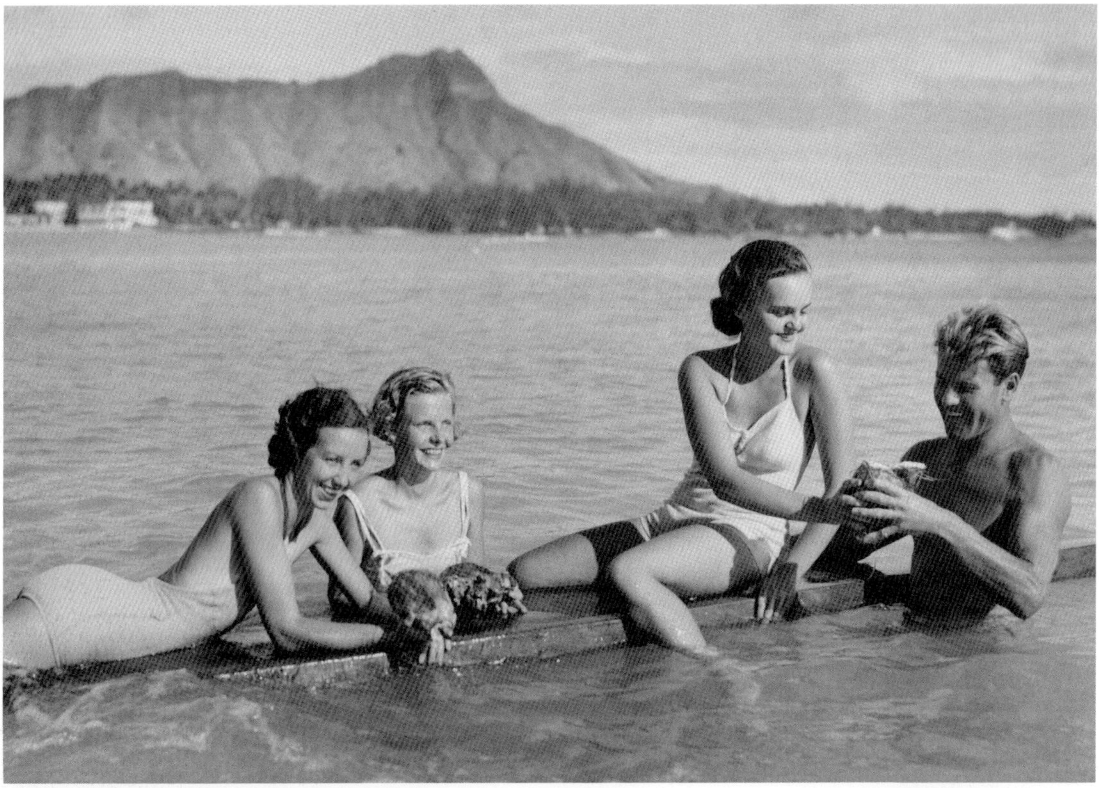

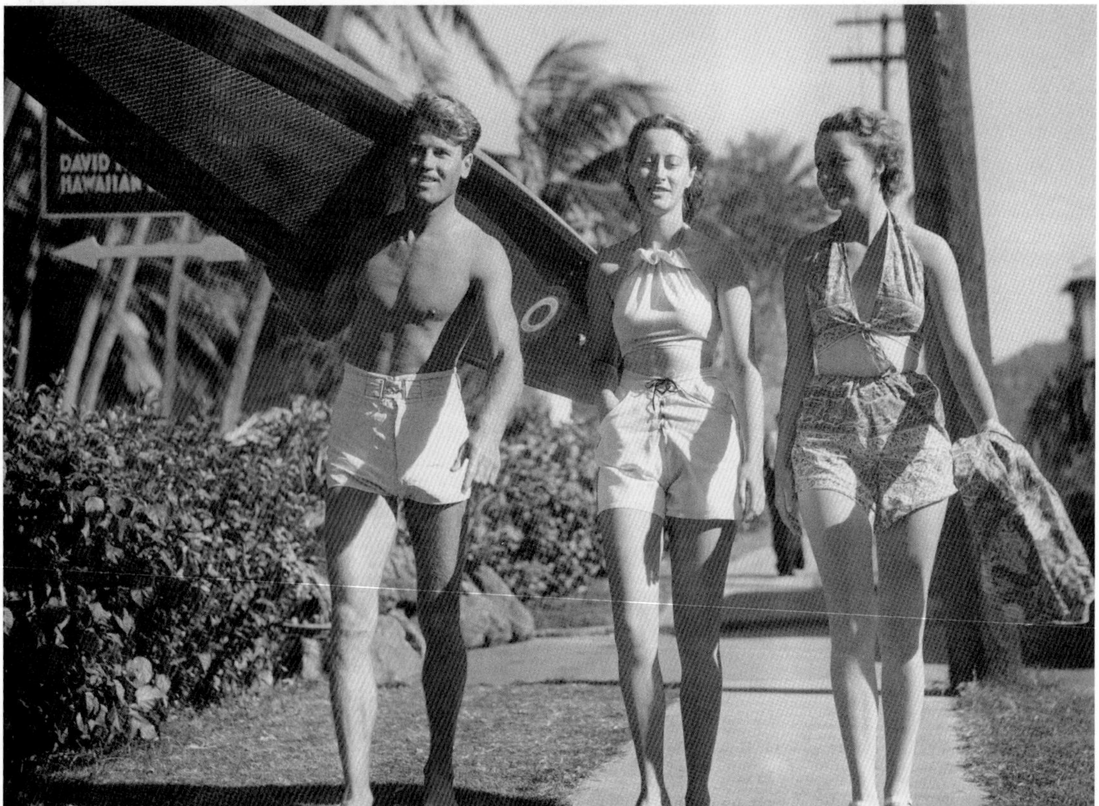
DAVID
HAWAIIAN

Photogenic Tom Blake was not only a real beachboy, but was handsome enough to be a model as well. These Pan-Pacific Press Bureau photos from the middle 1930s, distributed to publications throughout the U.S. to promote Hawai'i, make use of his good looks.

Facing page, above: Coconuts are served as a floating snack atop Tom's custom-built teak hollow board. **Below:** Tom hefts one of his innovative designs, this one manufactured by the Robert Mitchell company of Cincinnati, on a stroll along Kalākaua Avenue. Although over 12 feet long, it weighed only 44 pounds.

This page: Visiting singer Carl Brisson is escorted along the beach while carrying another of the Mitchell-manufactured boards. (All: N. R. Farbman)

Above & right: Tom Blake's contributions to surfboard design are significant. Intelligent and inquisitive, he researched traditional board construction by examining the historic collection at Bishop Museum and then worked to build lighter and more maneuverable examples than those currently in use. All the boards in these nearly identical photos, taken in late 1929 or early 1930, are his, and were specialized for surfing or paddling. The picture on the right has been published many times, but the one above is rarely seen, although it was first printed in the May 1935 *National Geographic*. *(Tom Blake)*

Above: As Tom Blake himself wrote in 1935, "When the surf fails to run at Waikiki one may see a surfboard rigged with a sail, skimming the bay before the trade winds...When the wind is right and [there's] no surf to ride, it is fun to sail this sporty outfit." Yet another of Tom's inventions was the sailboard. He first experimented with just a regular umbrella to catch the wind, but gradually refined the construction to what he's shown demonstrating here.
(N. R. Farbman)

Even while commercial companies were licensed to make and sell Blake-designed water equipment, the inventor himself also allowed do-it-yourself magazines to publish plans for his hollow surfboards. These were *Modern Mechanix* in 1933 and 1934, *Popular Mechanics* in 1937, and *Popular Science* in 1939 (reprinted in 1941). Here's one of Tom Blake's designs which was built on the island of Lāna'i in 1939, most likely based on the last article listed above. The photos show the surfboard's basic framework *(this page)* and the finished piece on the beach at Mānele Bay *(facing page)*.

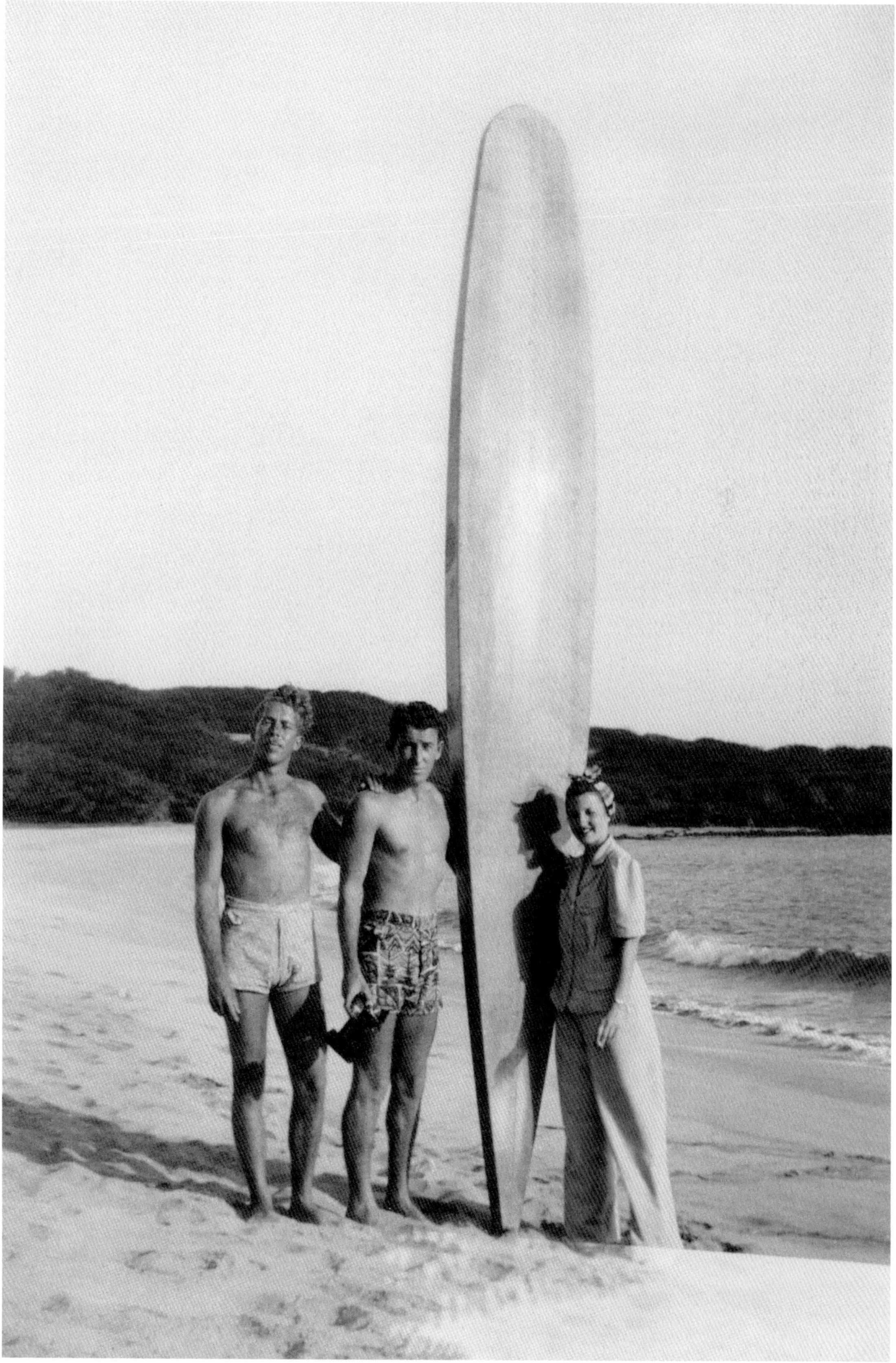

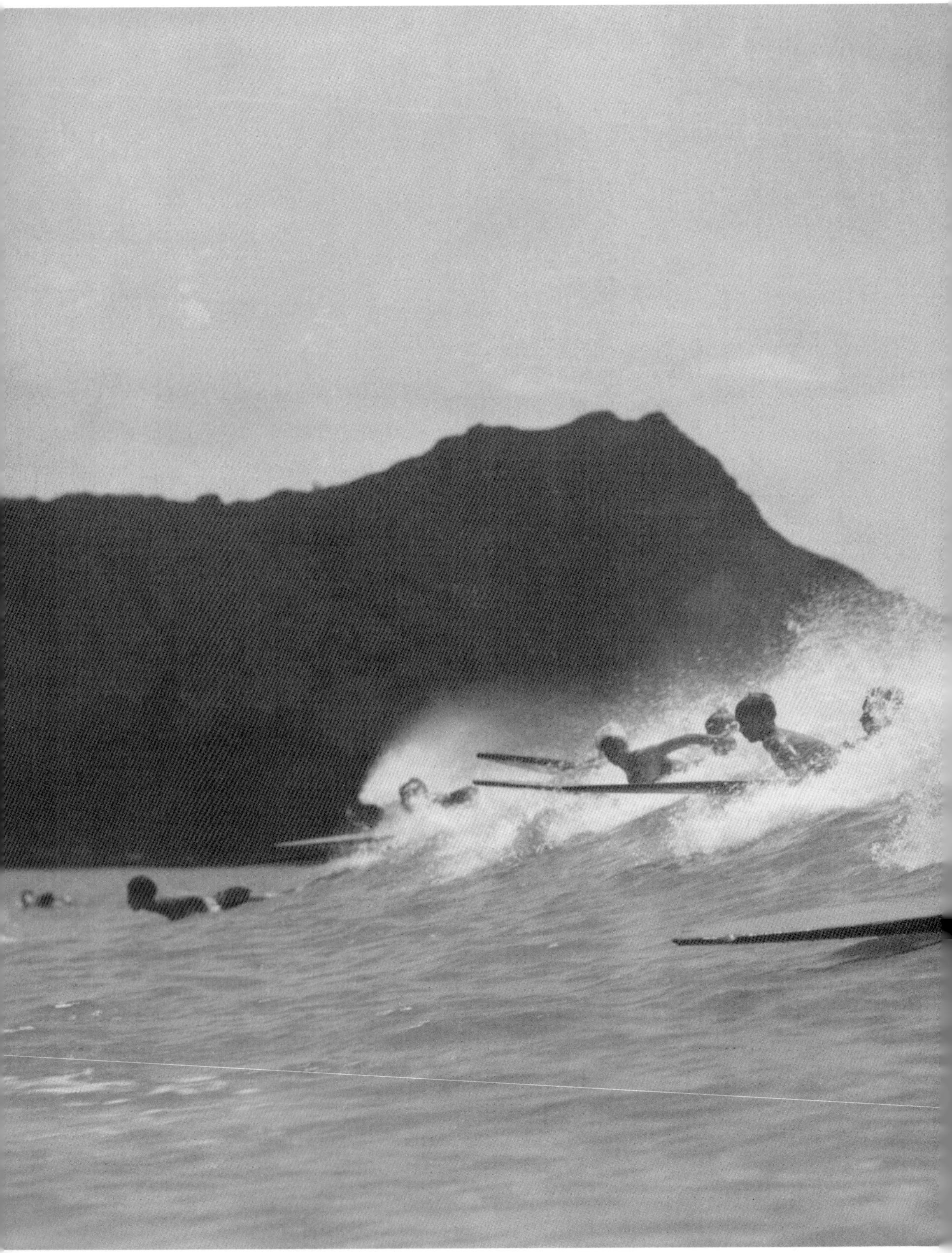

As if his other inventions were not enough, Tom Blake also was the first to build a waterproof camera housing in 1929, which he used to shoot a number of dynamic on-the-waves images at Waikīkī like the two on these pages. Both were among those published in his 1935 book, *Hawaiian Surfboard*. Some of the surfers in the photo above, from left, are beachboy Hawkshaw (John Pahia, in white hat, 2nd), Babe Gillespie (3rd), and Virginia Hammond (in white bathing cap, 4th). Blake himself donated this photo to Bishop Museum in 1931. *(Tom Blake)*

[75

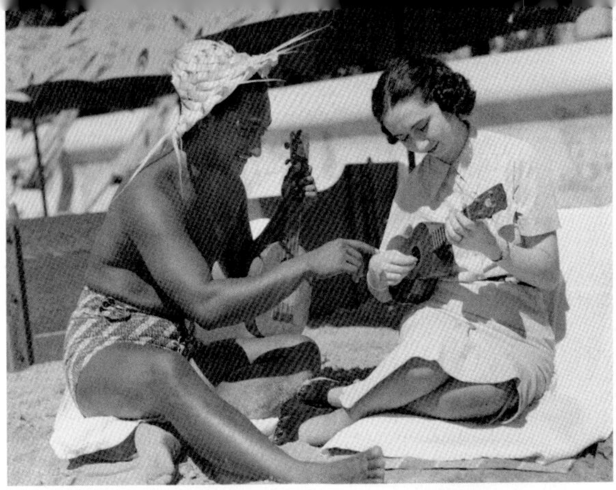
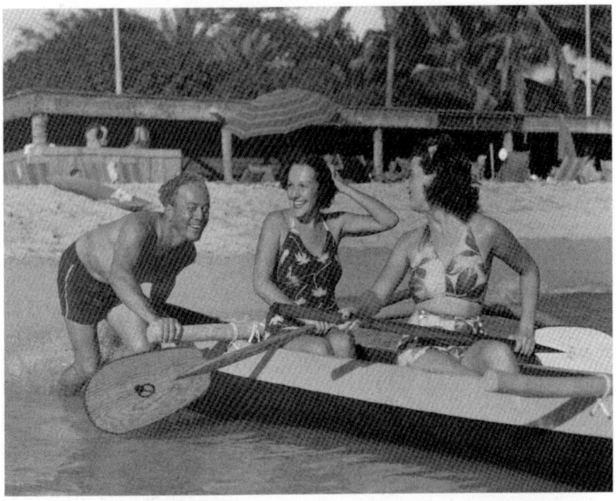
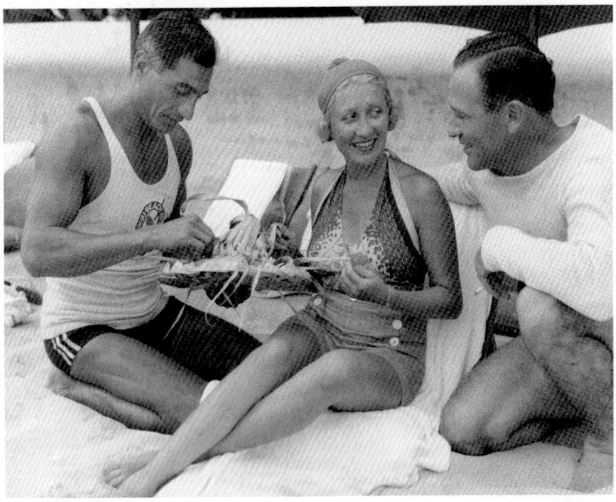
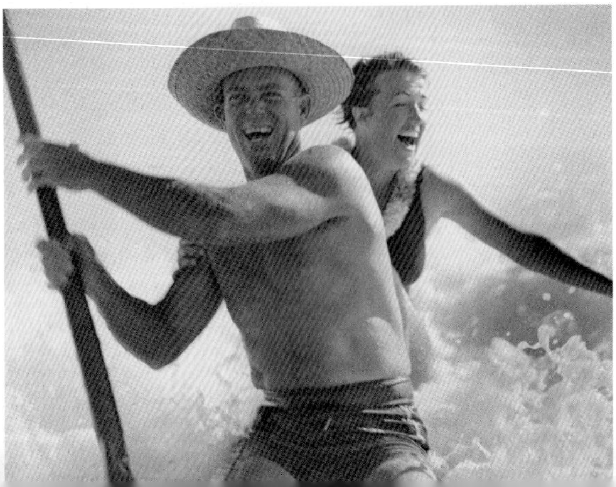
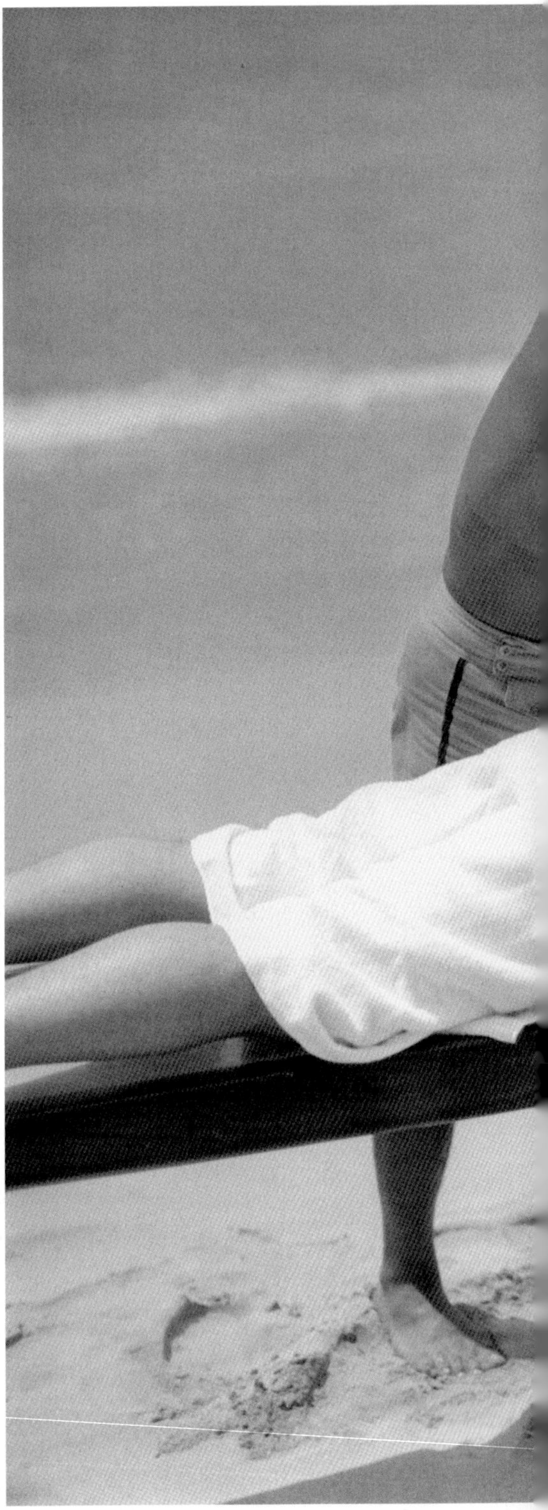

Beachboys were an integral part of Waikīkī's fame. They provided services of all kinds to tourists, some of whom developed close friendships with them. All these photographs were taken between 1934 and 1937 by Nate Farbman for the Pan-Pacific Press Bureau, and were intended to publicize Hawai'i in mainland newspapers and magazines. *(N. R. Farbman)*

In the 1930s, vacationing movie stars cooperated in posing for publicity pictures at Waikīkī, like these. **This page, above:** Mary Pickford, once "America's Sweetheart" but by this time retired from films, stands with Georgie Kepoo while on her honeymoon with Charles "Buddy" Rogers in 1936. *(N. R. Farbman)* **Right:** Mickey Rooney shoulders a surfboard in front of the Royal Hawaiian Hotel.
Facing page: Eddie Cantor was a popular comedian who appeared in movies but at this time was even better known for his national radio program. *(N. R. Farbman)*

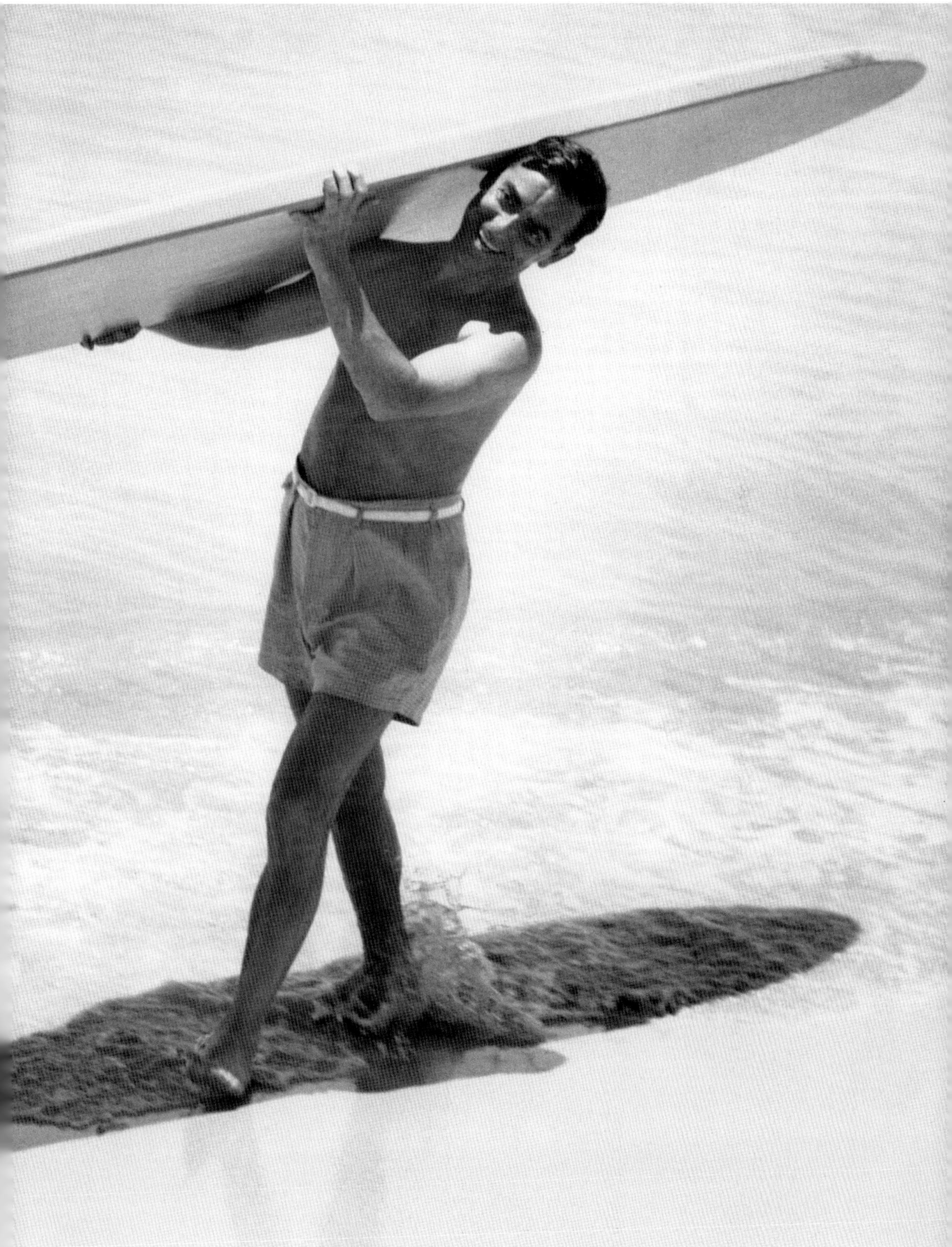

This page, above: Bing Crosby pretends to play a steel guitar while beachboy Panama Dave stands over his shoulder. **Right:** Jeanette MacDonald, famous for her operatic singing in a number of musical films, sits on a canoe flanked by two beachboys, including Sally Hale at left. *(N. R. Farbman)*

Facing page: In August 1935, Shirley Temple and her mother prepare to depart for Los Angeles after the little star's first visit. With them is the special surfboard she received from the beachboys of the Waikiki Beach Patrol.

ALOHA
Capt. Shirley

Postcards in the 1930s continued to feature surfing as an immediately recognized symbol of Hawai'i.

Top left: Roy Craw, Jr. is the nearest surfer in this hand-colored card published by the Sunny Scenes company of Florida.

Top right: This image was photographed by Tom Blake, and when published in his 1935 book *Hawaiian Surfboard* its original caption read, "The surf at Waikiki is not as mean as the surf of the mainland United States except at certain places. It sweeps shoreward offering a perfect ride to the outrigger canoe and surfer." *(Tom Blake)*

82]

Below: The stability of a large board allows this man to stand comfortably upright with little need to maneuver his body.

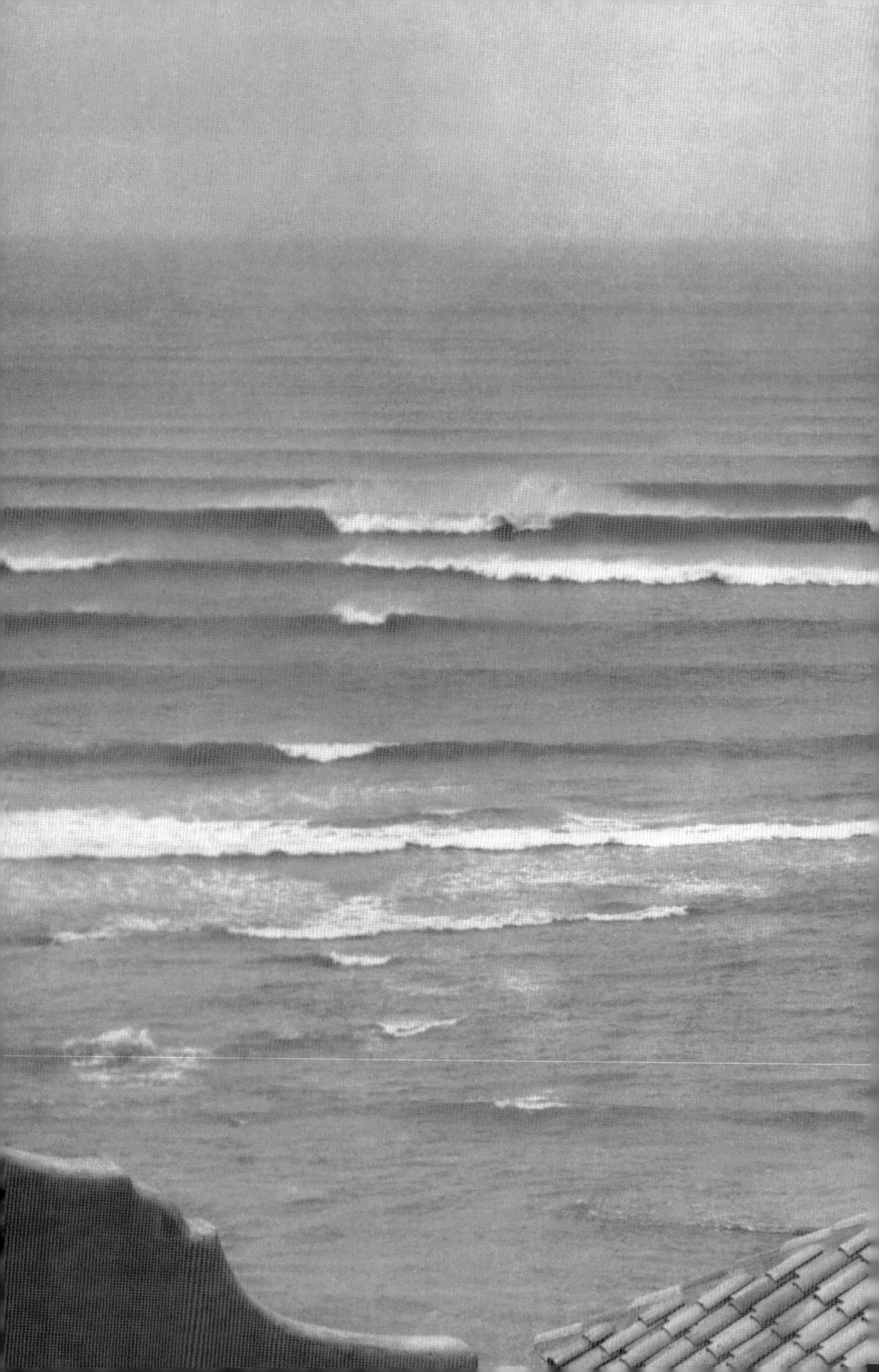

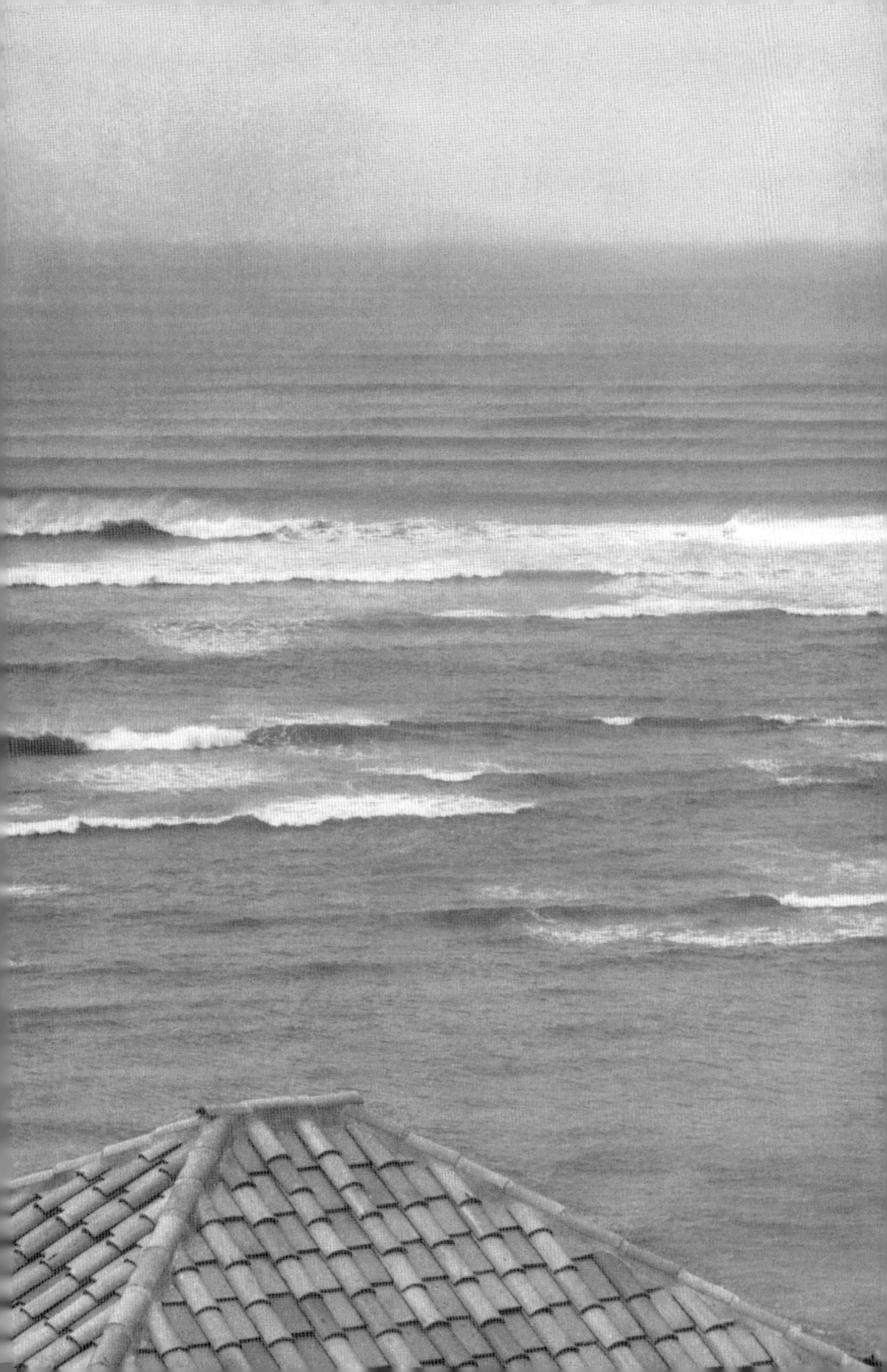

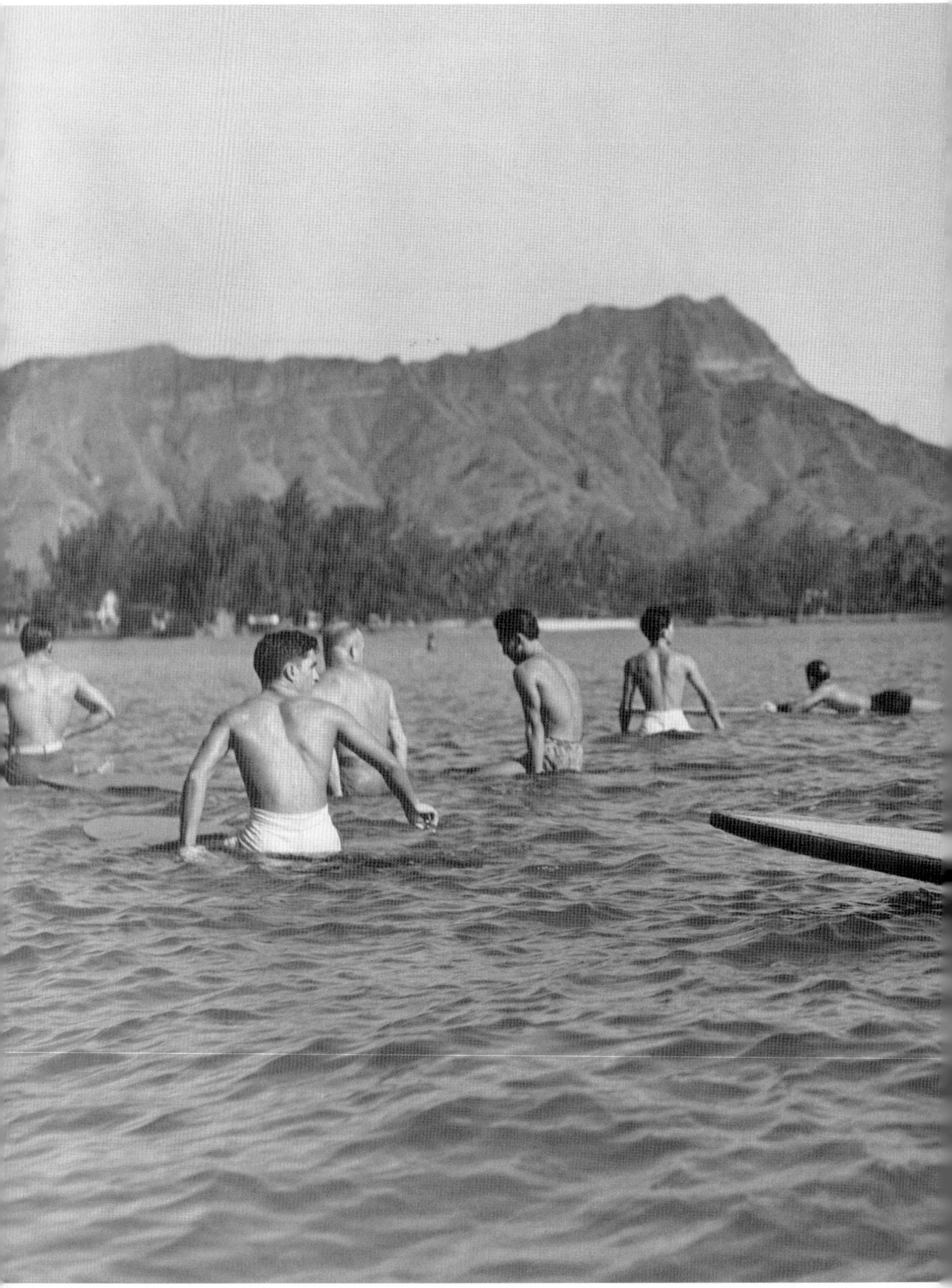

Previous pages: Tom Blake photographed this impressive Waikīkī surf from the roof of the Royal Hawaiian Hotel in the early 1930s. The lines of incoming waves appear to be continuous from left to right to an untrained observer, yet they actually comprise a number of different named breaks which have different characteristics. *(Tom Blake)*

Left: Surfers are always at the mercy of the ocean, and sometimes there are no waves, even if you sit and stare out to sea in anticipation.
Above: At such times, the prepared surfer brings along a book to kill time while waiting for the water to cooperate. *(Both: N. R. Farbman)*

Below: Surfboards are lined up at the Outrigger Canoe Club's canoe storage pavilion at Waikiki in about 1938. Visible at the base of the nearest one is the logo of the Swastika Surf-Board Company, a subsidiary of Pacific System Homes Inc. of Los Angeles. Although not generally known today, the swastika was used by different cultures for centuries and came to be considered a sort of good luck emblem. But after the Nazis took power in Germany in 1934, it became a notorious symbol of oppression and hatred. The company was thus forced to drop the swastika in 1939, becoming (far more appropriately) the Waikiki Surf-Board Company. Regardless of symbols, the business was proud to advertise that their surfboards were "selected by the world-famous Outrigger Canoe Club of Waikiki Beach, Honolulu, T.H., as the official Board of this renowned organization." This photo shows that claim to be true. *(William Pitchford)*

Above: From 1935 to 1941, the United States government claimed possession of three tiny islands near the equator (Baker, Jarvis, and Howland islands) by stationing groups of young Hawaiian men on them. The men, mostly graduates of the Kamehameha School, usually stayed for periods of several months at a time. Their best-known activities were the futile preparations for aviator Amelia Earhart's planned landing on Howland Island in 1937 in the last stages of her around-the-world flight; Earhart disappeared en route, and her fate is still debated. The entire colonization process ended when the Japanese attacked the islands at the start of World War II, and the survivors were fortunately rescued early in 1942.

Without much to do, four colonists of Jarvis Island in 1935 went surfing, as this photo shows. The story is that they built these boards themselves, but were forced to give them up when the overseeing military officers visited on one of the regular runs by a Coast Guard ship. Apparently it was feared they could be injured in the ocean, and medical help was over a thousand miles away. *(William T. Miller)*

The U.S. went through a Hawaiian craze in the late 1930s, which was initially inspired by the popularity of a Hollywood musical called *Waikiki Wedding*, released in 1937. Most of the film was made on sets at Paramount Pictures, but a few location shots did make their way into the final edit. A number of these incidental scenes were filmed at Nānākuli, where a group of surfers took to the water, as shown here. In the movie, they can only be seen briefly as background for the opening credits. *(N. R. Farbman)*

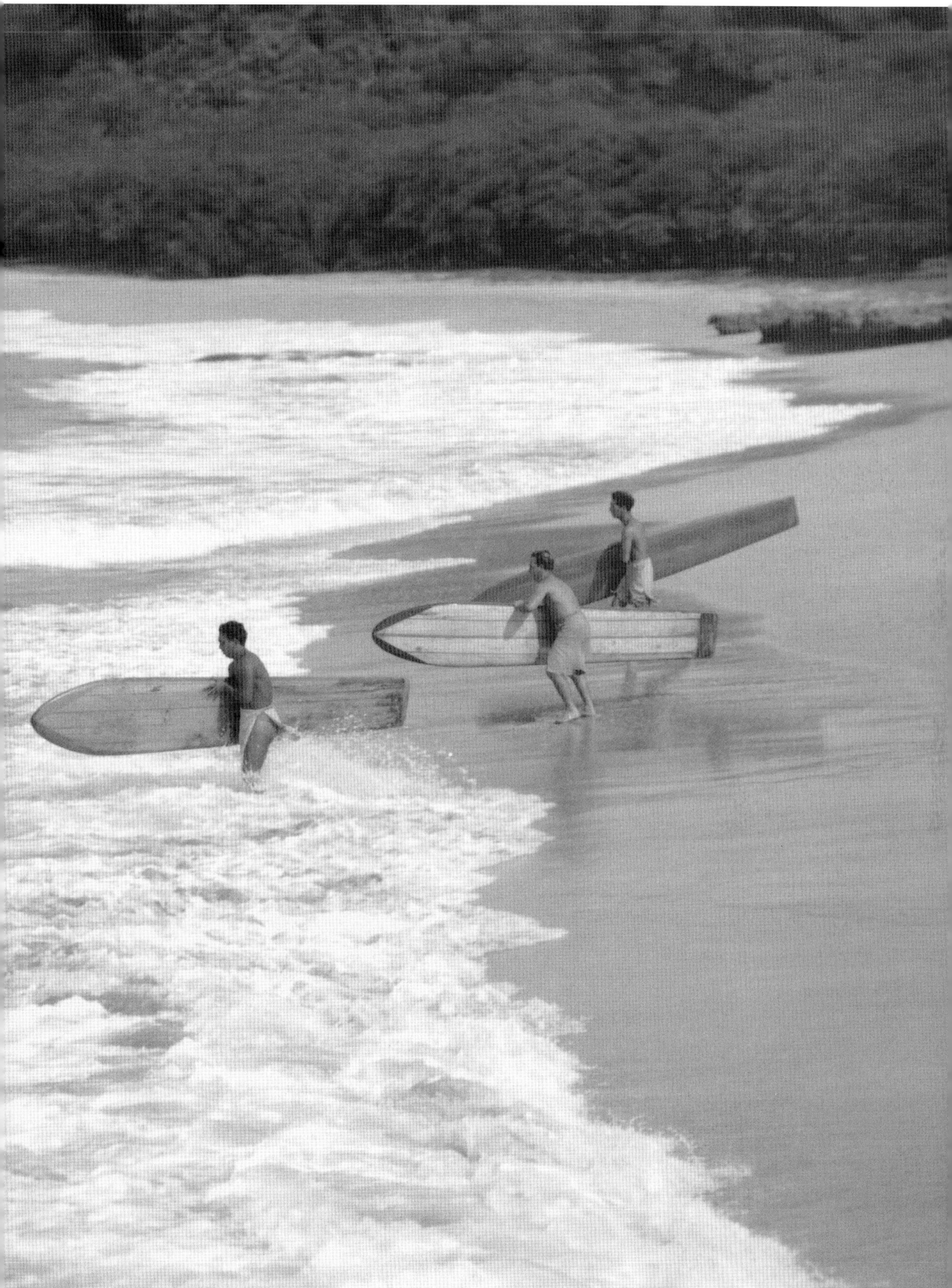

All of these pictures were sold commercially as souvenirs in about 1940. At that time, people still kept scrapbooks where they would glue in their own snapshots, as well as photos that they purchased, like these.

This page, above: A man with a large surfboard is intentionally posed at Kuhio Beach with the Royal Hawaiian and Moana Hotels in the background. **Below:** A surfer stands near the dining room of the Moana Hotel (at left).

Facing page: A young Hawaiian man with a well-used board, whose splintered prow shows evidence of some collisions.

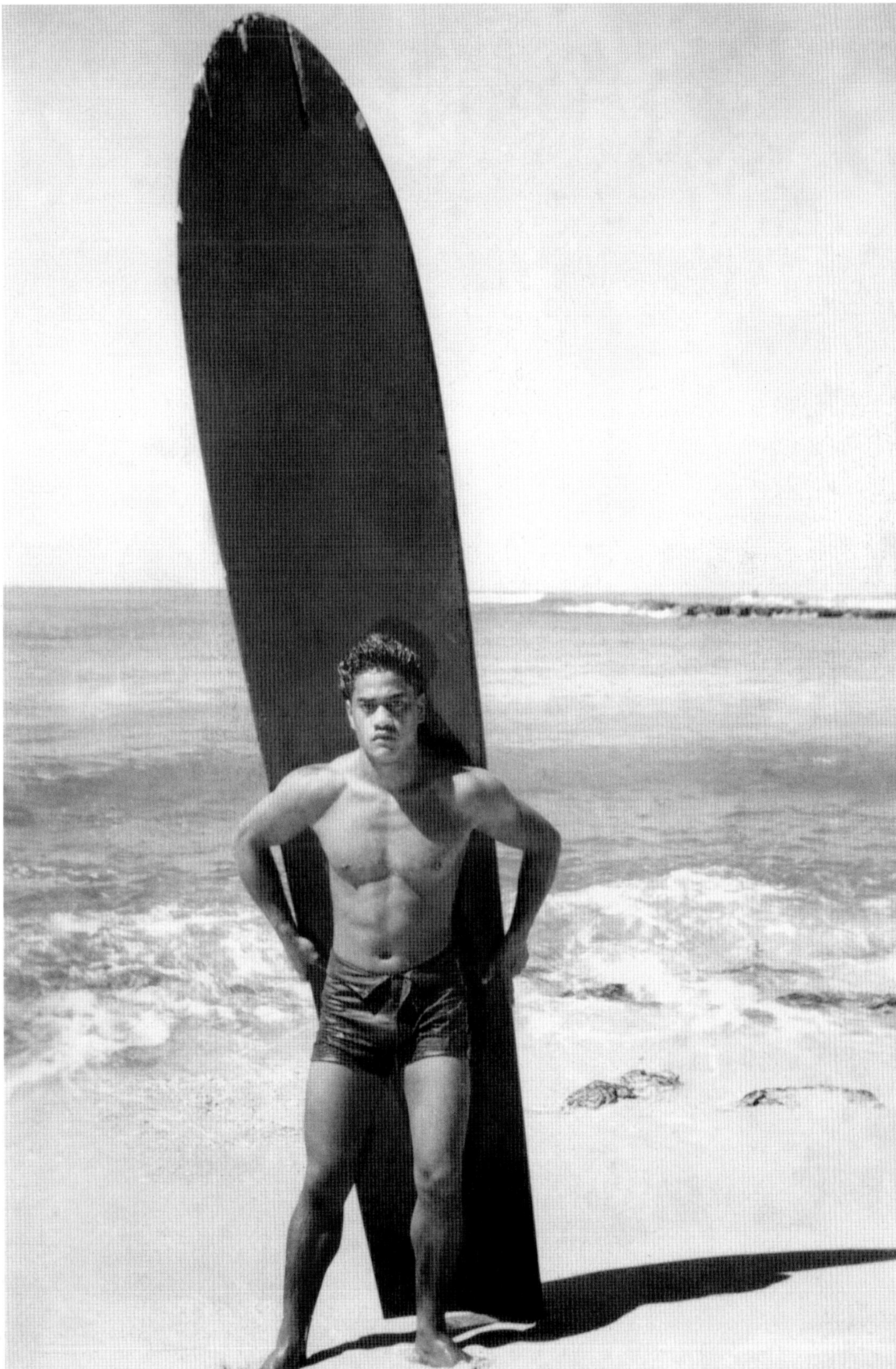

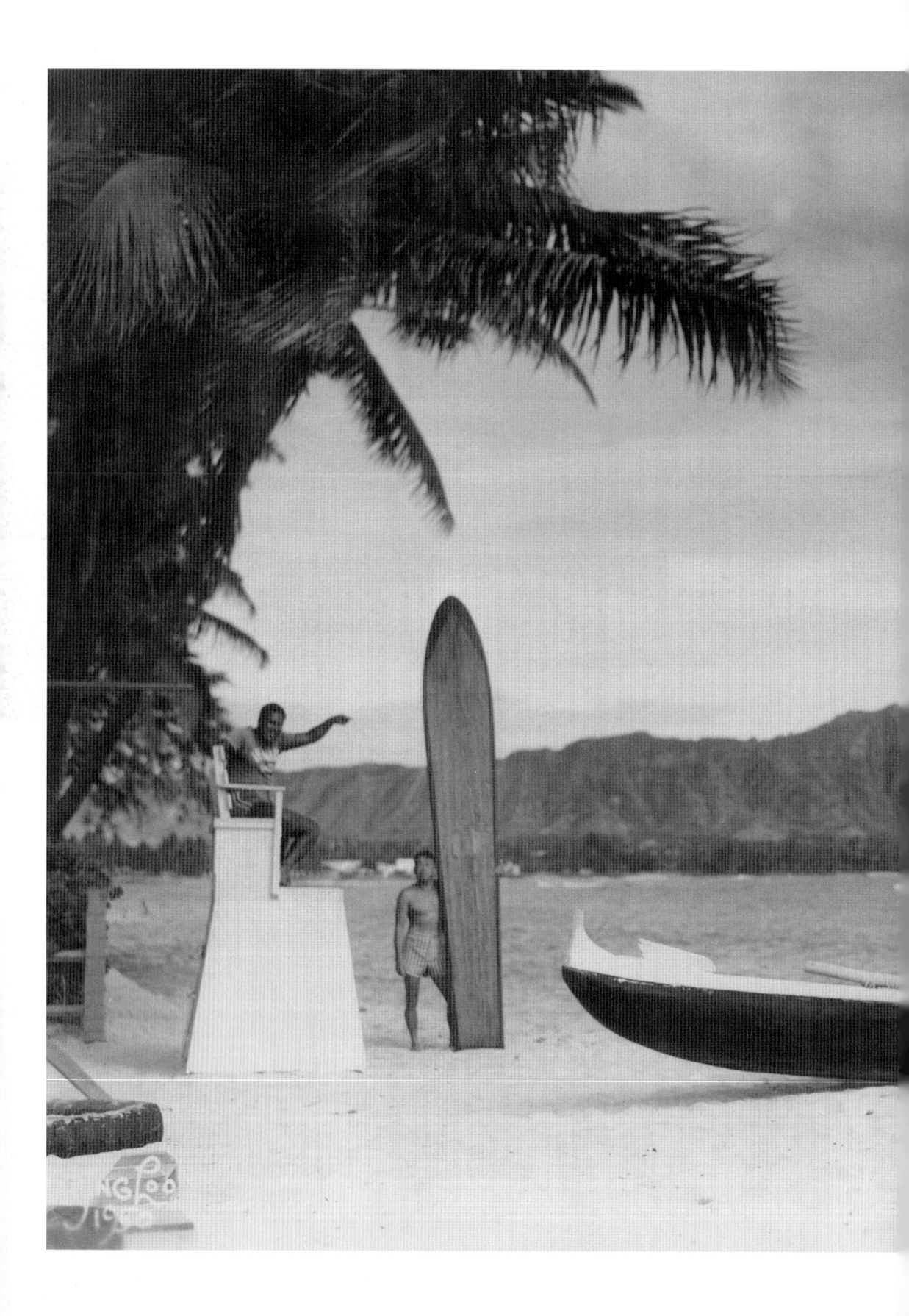

Surfboards continue to appear as props to add an unmistakable Hawaiian touch to photographs in the 1950s. (*Left: Tai Sing Loo; above: Laurence Hata Collection*)

Following pages: Surfin' Santa arrives at Waikīkī in about 1955. (*Irving Rosen*)

[95]

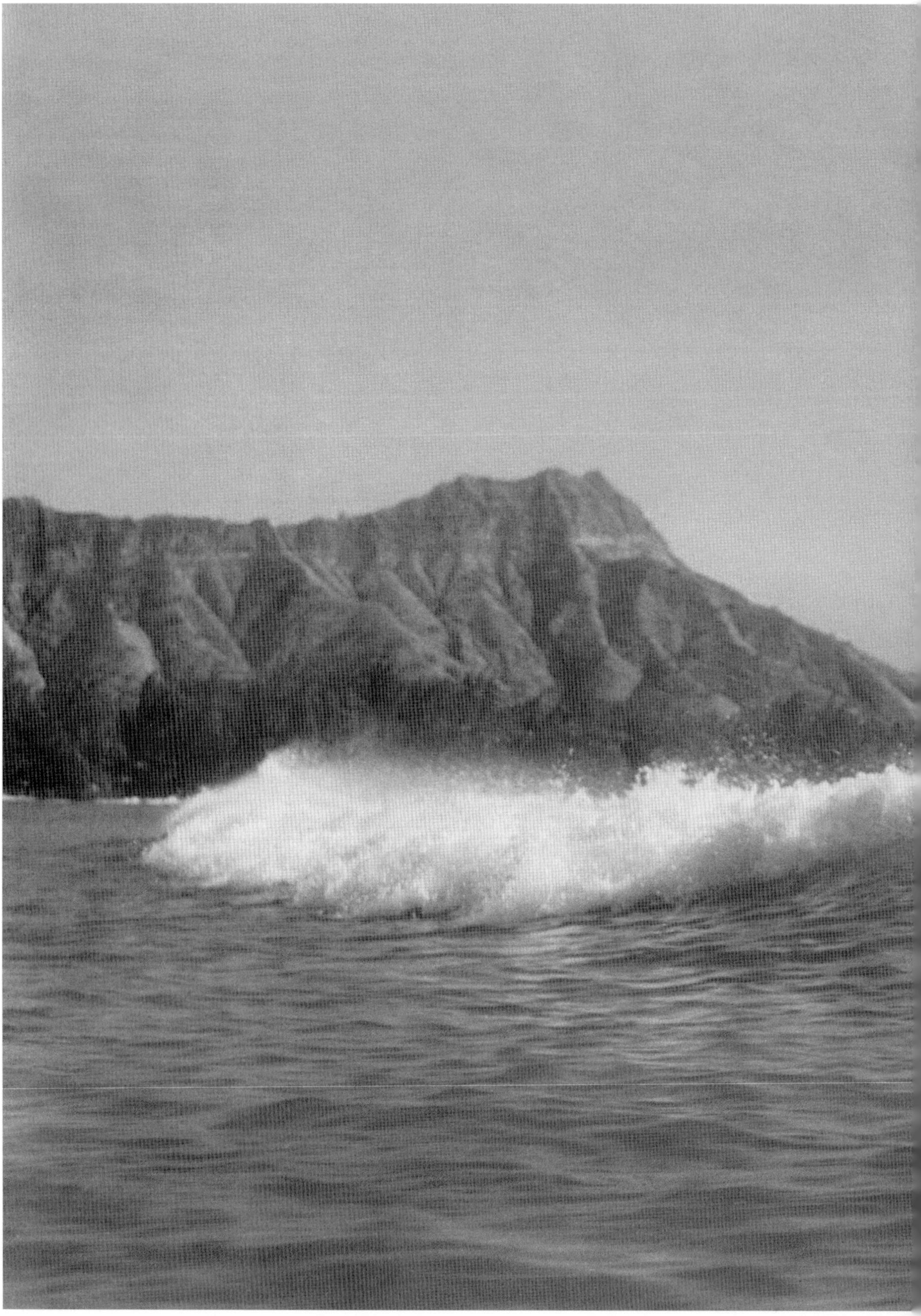

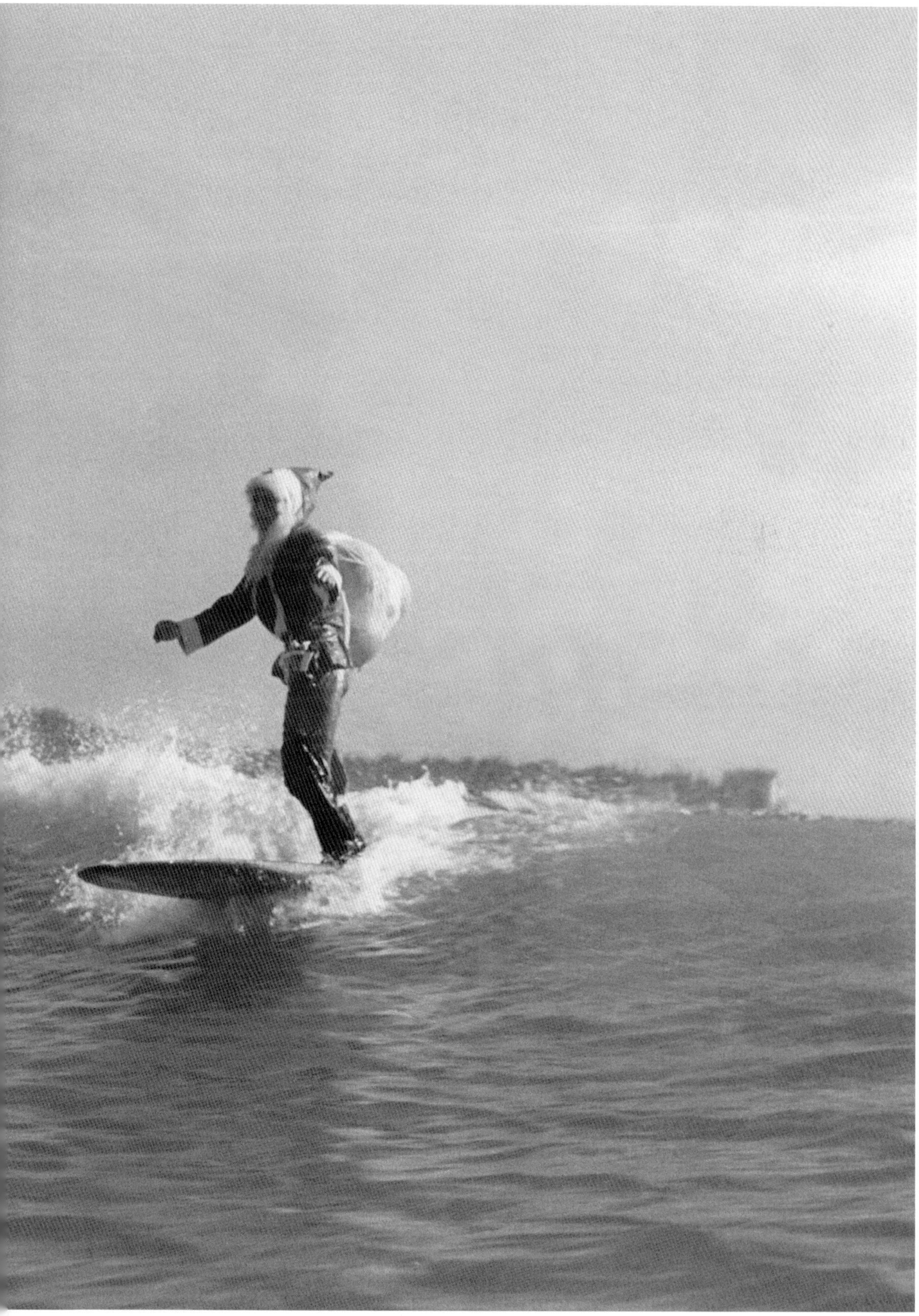

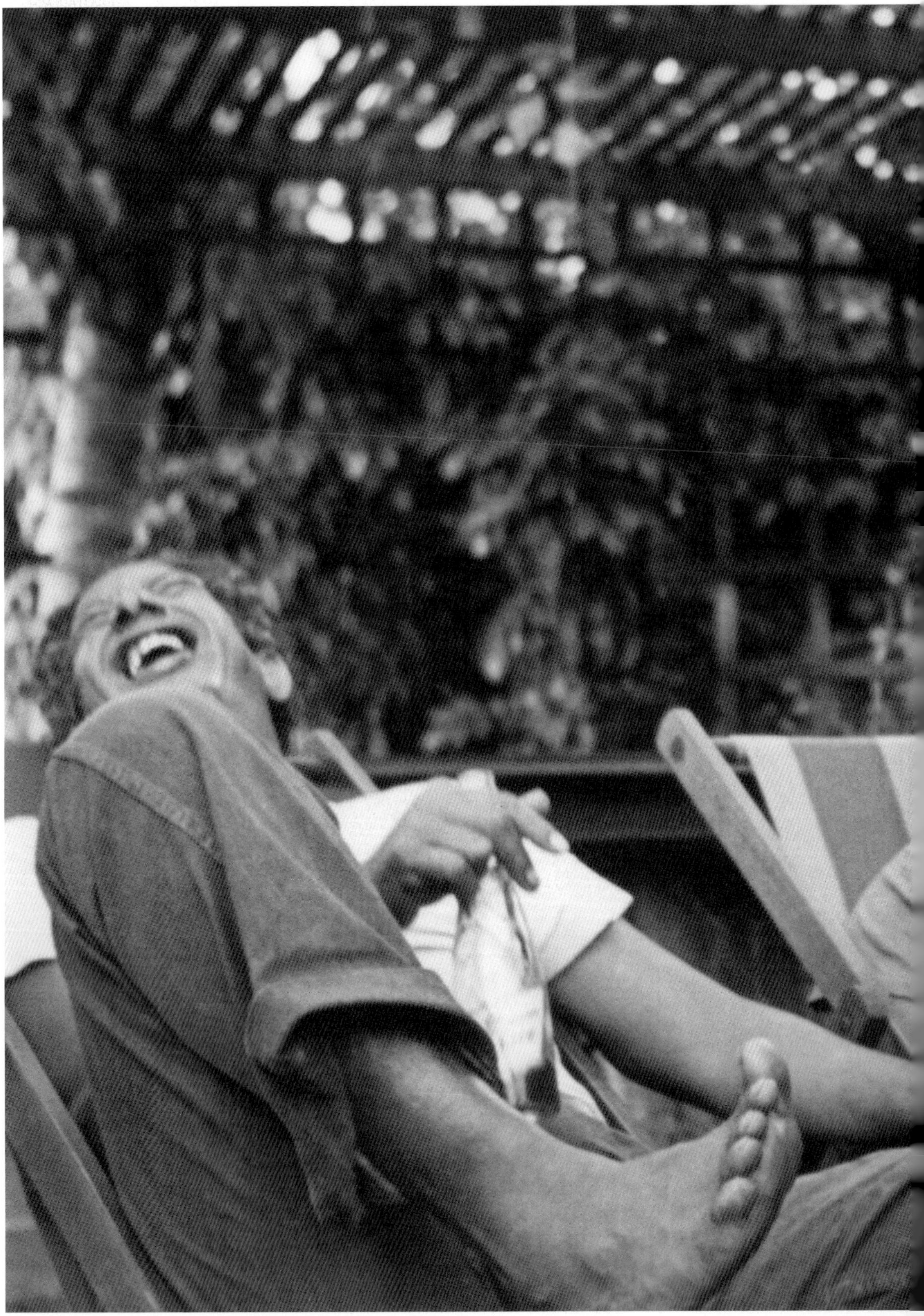

Beachboys were usually thought of as happy-go-lucky playboys. They were expected to provide amusement for beach-going tourists, and showing a visitor a particularly good time might lead to rewards like a substantial tip, an expensive gift, or even a trip to the mainland. There were always tourists eager to cut loose, and accommodating their wishes led to a life of semi-continuous partying for some beachboys. In the end, though, that wasn't always fun. Regardless of the eventual consequences, here are "Tough Bill" Keaweamahi on the left and Chick Daniels on the right raising a little hell at a backyard booze-up around 1950.

In the 1950s came the gradual increase of what would be known as the surfer lifestyle—young men choosing mainly to surf, party sometimes (or often), and live cheaply wherever they could be close to the ocean. By 1962, there were enough people like this for the derogatory term "surf bum" to appear. But "bum" or not, one necessity for any surfer was a car that could carry a surfboard (or boards). Of necessity, this had to be inexpensive (and was therefore old), and in fact the more antiquated and worn-out the vehicle was, the prouder the owner might be. Seen here are some surf mobiles in use.

Above: Surfer cars (note the one at far right) are parked near the Hawaiian Village Hotel in 1958 while their owners take in the last waves of the day at Kaiser's or Rock Pile. The construction of this hotel's enclosed lagoon a few years earlier had resulted in this filled-in piece of land, which pushed the shoreline outwards some distance. The nearby surf break had been named after the man responsible for the project, wealthy industrialist Henry J. Kaiser. *(Laurence Hata)*

Right: Cruising down Kalākaua Avenue in 1960 is this nineteen-year-old '41 Plymouth convertible, whose lack of a back window easily accommodates two surfboards. *(Laurence Hata Collection)*

[101

Above: Mrs. George Lage, a mainland visitor, poses with a beachboy and his surfboard at Waikīkī in November 1959. His tank top and trunks bear the logo of the Outrigger Beach Services. A 1950s promotional brochure for this organization proudly announced that it had "a staff of trained men skilled in this sport. You may arrange to have one of them take you surfboarding. Try it! Warning: You may become an addict."

Right: Canoe paddling, like surfing, was a tradition that carried on strongly and continues undiminished today. This scene is from about 1950.

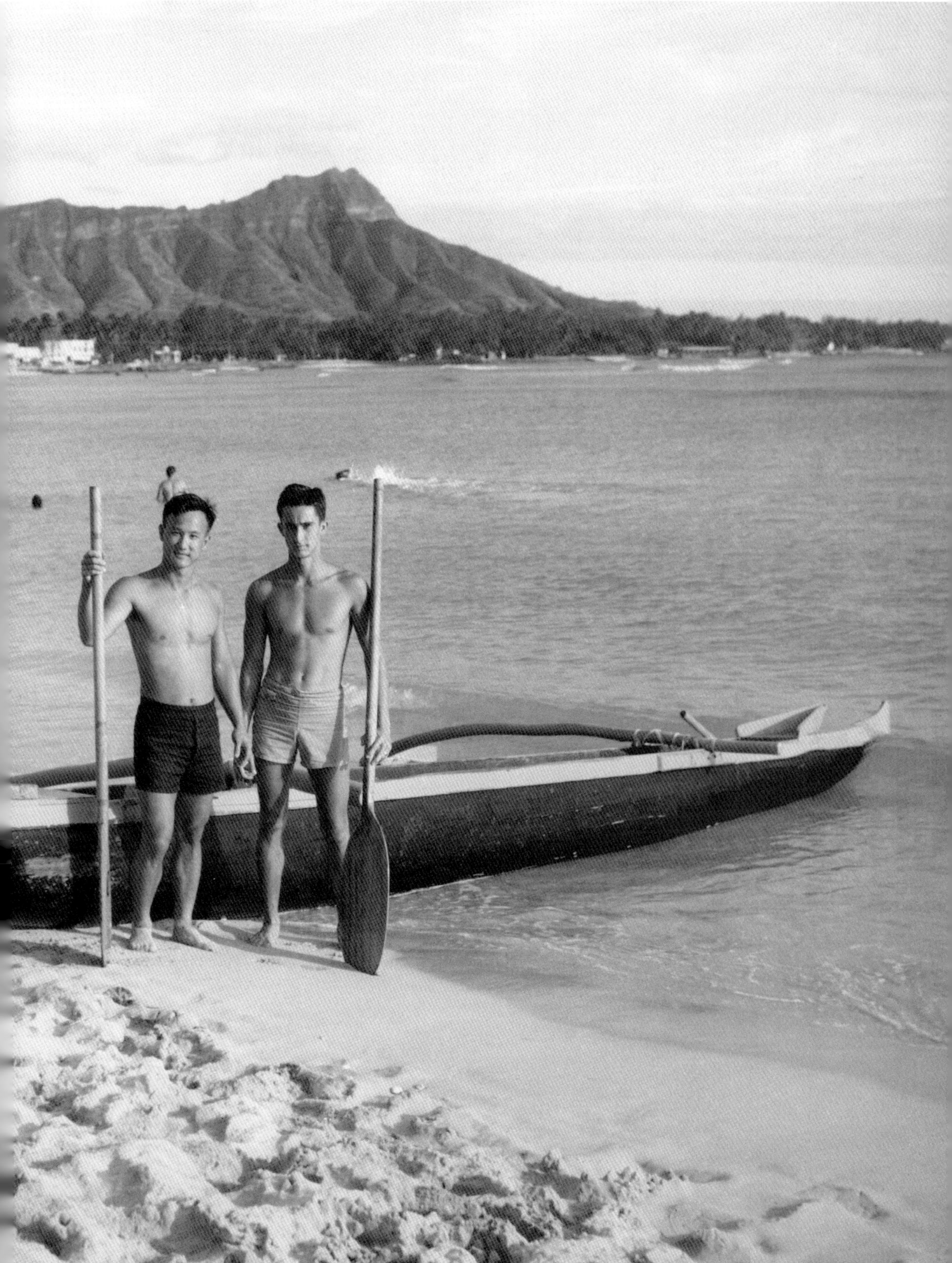

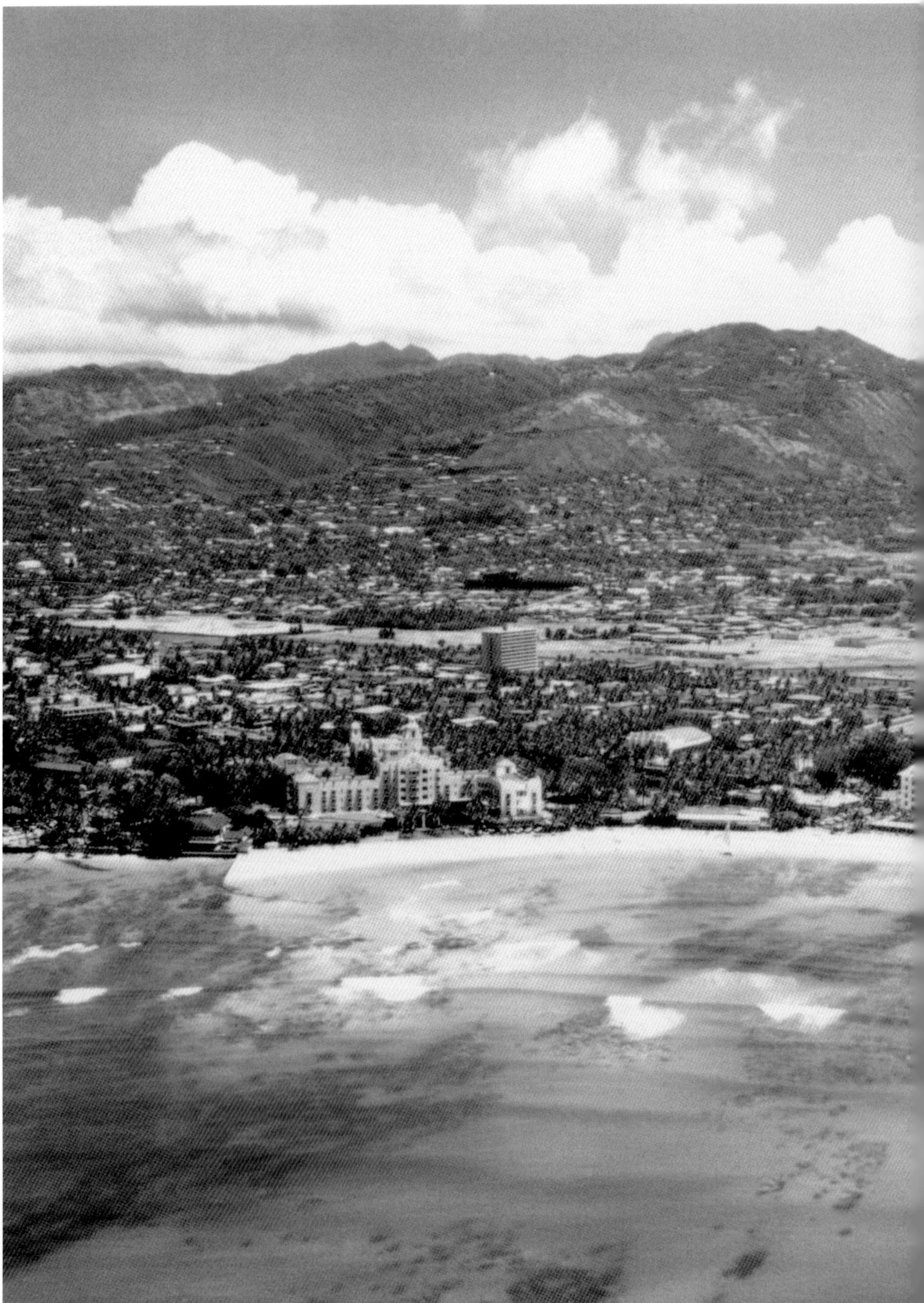

Left: An aerial view of Waikīkī shortly just after 1955. A few new highrises have just appeared: the Rosalei apartments in the distance above the Royal Hawaiian, the Princess Ka'iulani Hotel above the Moana, and the Biltmore Hotel on the right. The surf, however, rolls in unchanged. *(Laurence Hata)*

Above: Fun on the beach in front of the Outrigger Canoe Club, with the Royal Hawaiian Hotel's dining room in the distance, around 1955. *(Laurence Hata)*

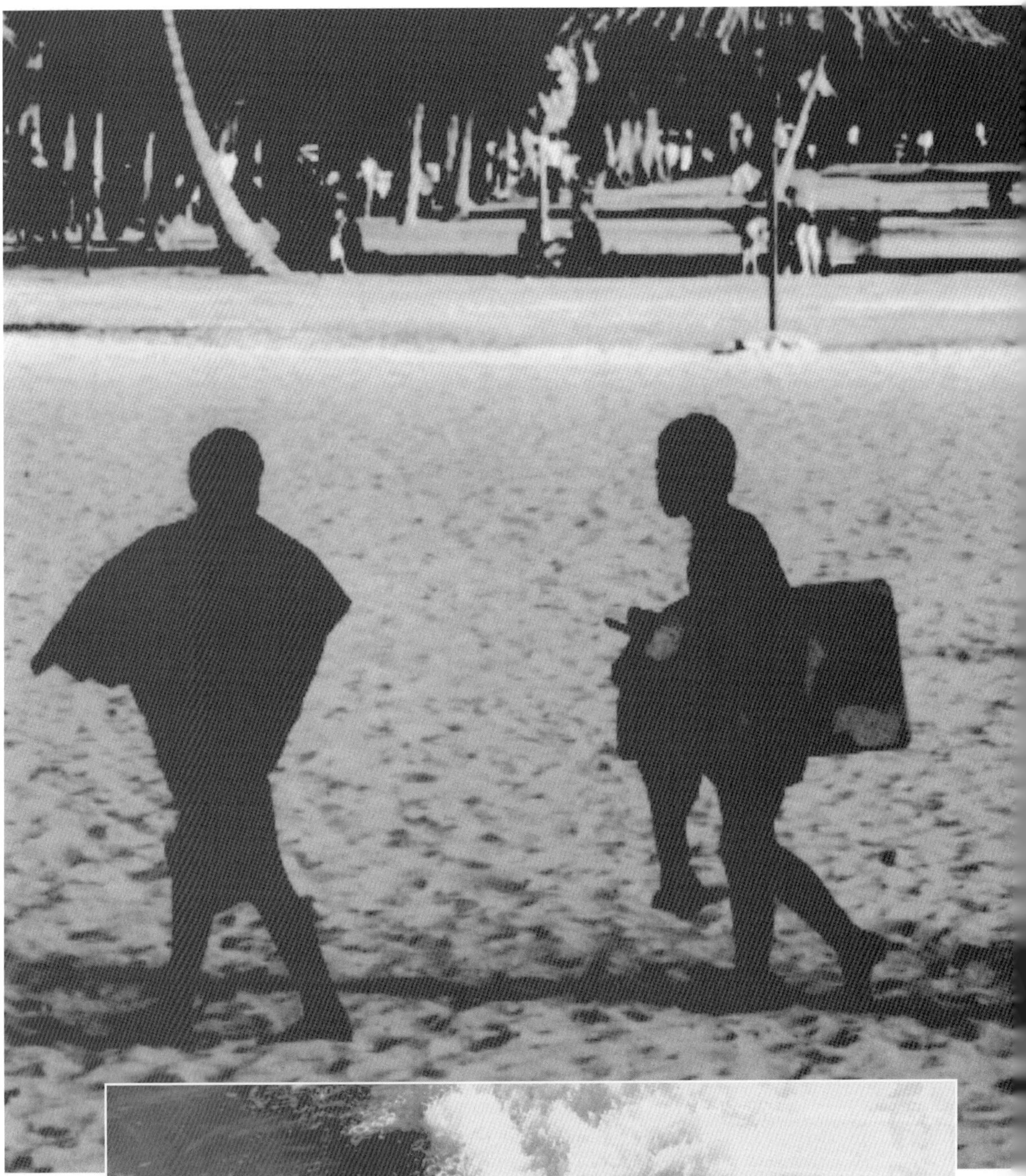

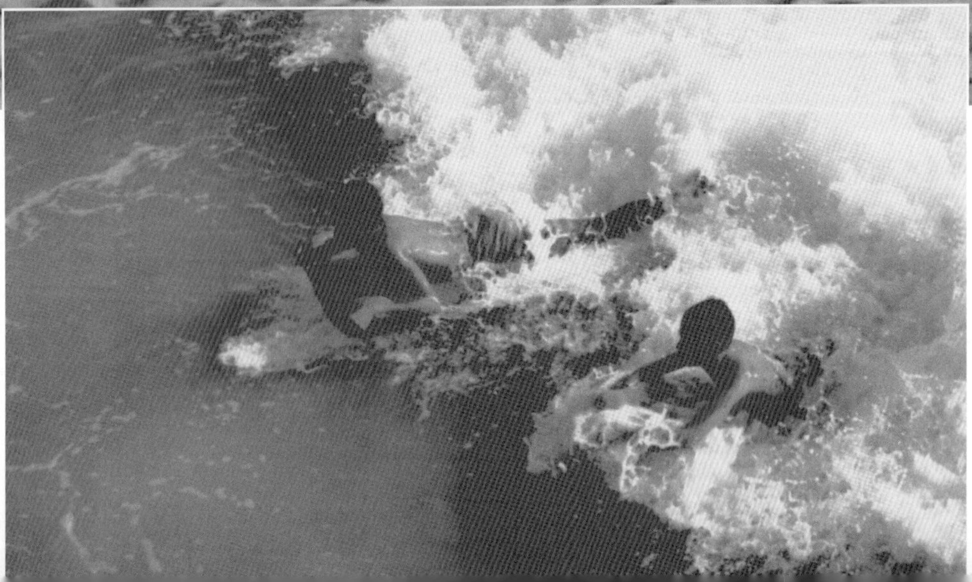

Above: Full-sized longboards got most of the attention for many years, but they weren't the whole story. For one thing, smaller boards served very well for smaller people, as shown by these boys at Waikīkī in the late 1950s. One carries an inflated mat, while the others have simple homemade plywood boards known by that time as "paipo boards." The derivation of this term, according to surf historian John Clark, comes from a now-archaic Hawaiian word for bodysurfing: *paepo*. Although it's now forgotten, the term was still in use in the 1930s and '40s, and gradually came to be applied to this type of small board, although with its spelling and pronunciation changed. *(Laurence Hata)*

Left: The Kapahulu Groin, a pier-like concrete structure housing a drainage outfall, was constructed in the early 1950s just opposite the intersection where Kapahulu Avenue ends at Kalākaua Avenue. It soon became a favorite place for kids to swim, jump from, and surf next to. These young surfers were photographed there around 1960. *(Laurence Hata)*

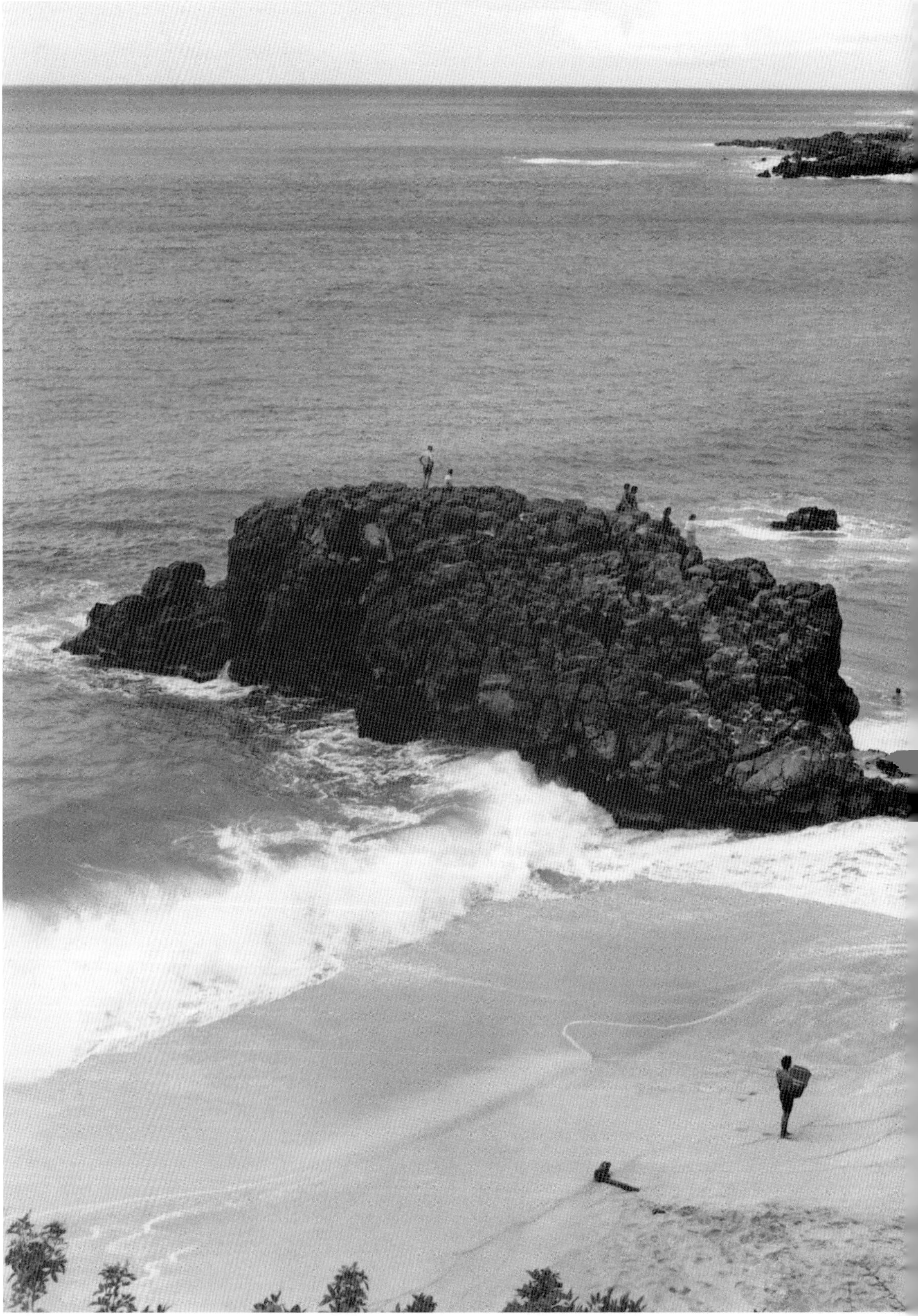

Left: The wash of the ocean at Waimea Bay leaves a thin, slick layer of water for these guys to go sand sliding about around 1960. Waves may not be involved, but this qualifies as a form of surfing nonetheless. *(Laurence Hata)*
Above: Along the Wai'anae coast in the middle 1960s, bodysurfers are engulfed in a steep, sudden break. *(Laurence Hata)*

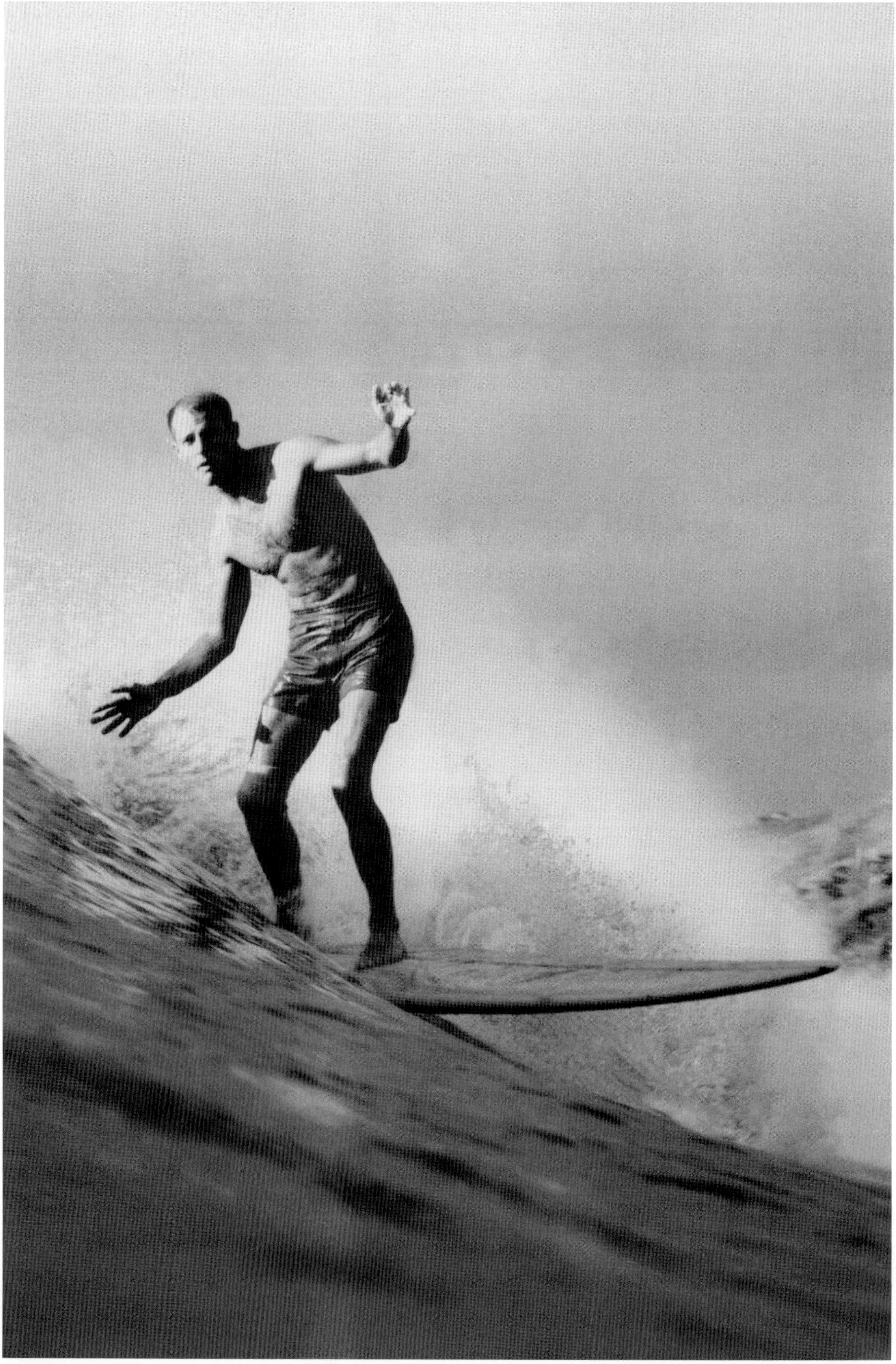

These photos were taken in the 1960s, when surfing had exploded into an international fad. In previous decades the sport had been associated almost exclusively with Hawai'i, but its sudden growth in California shifted the focus there. Overnight, there was surf music and surf clothing, skateboarding (or "sidewalk surfing," as the Jan and Dean song of 1964 called it), and lightweight "beach party" movies from Hollywood. Hawai'i was still acknowledged as the home of surfing, but its status was somewhat overshadowed. Any or all of the photos on these two pages may have been released by the Hawaii Visitors Bureau in the '60s to promote Hawai'i through the time-tested appeal of surfing, which was heightened in that decade by the aforementioned fad. *(Laurence Hata Collection)*

[111]

Below: Waikīkī offshore in the middle 1960s, with a mix of boys and girls on the lighter foam and fiberglass boards that nearly anyone could use. Newspaper complaints of overcrowding had started as early as 1956 and soon increased, as in this 1963 headline: "Waikiki Has 3 Times As Many Surfers As Area Can Safely Handle."

Right: Waikīkī from the air in about 1962. On the beach itself, from the left, are the Moana Hotel, the Surfrider Hotel, the Waikiki Bowl (a bowling alley, soon to be demolished), and the newly-built Waikiki Beach Center changing rooms. (In turn, this structure too would be demolished in the 1990s.) Visible in the ocean are numerous surfers and canoes; the growth of tourism, spurred by jet travel (which began in 1959) was about to kick Waikīkī into uncontrolled growth. *(All: Laurence Hata)*

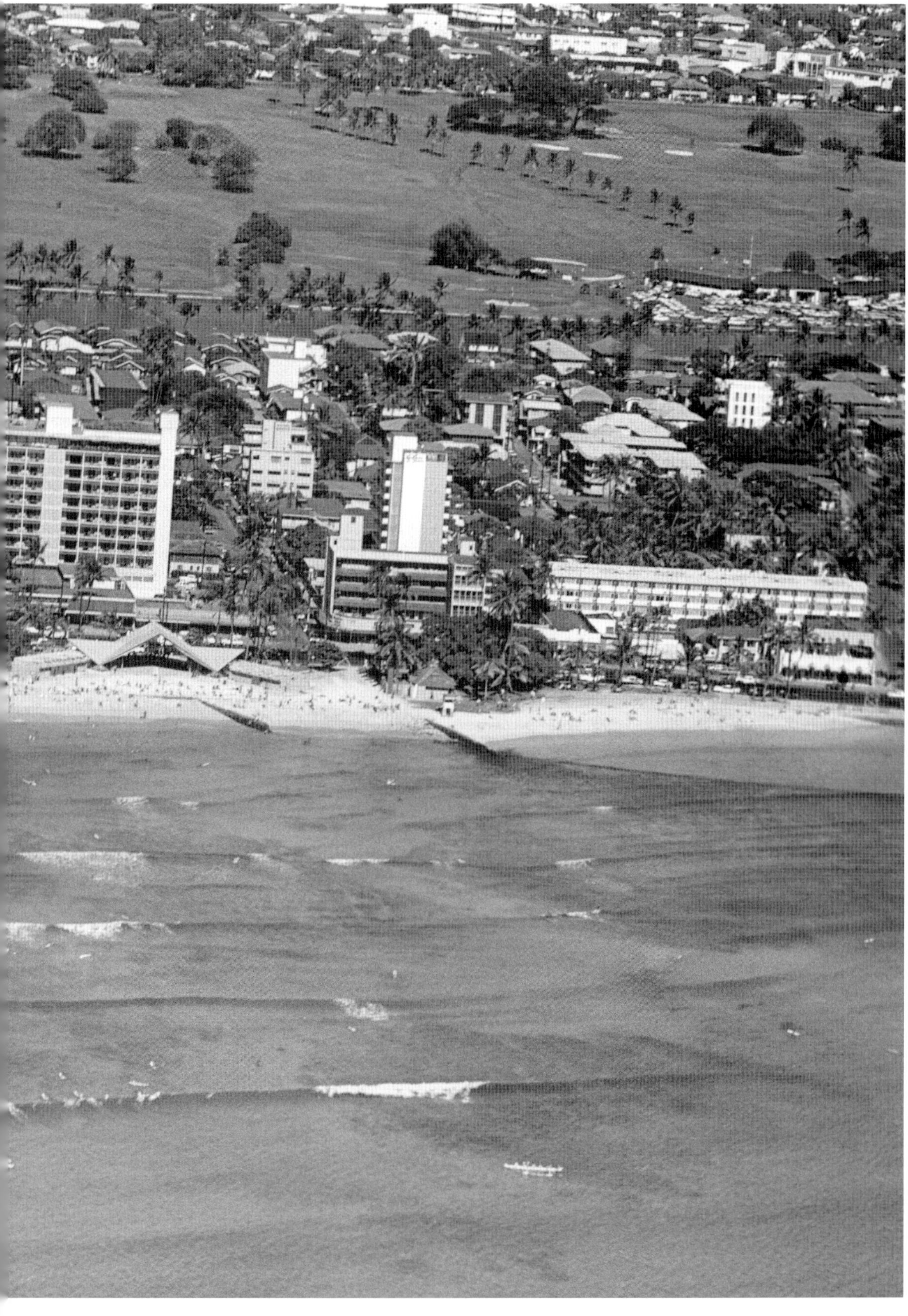

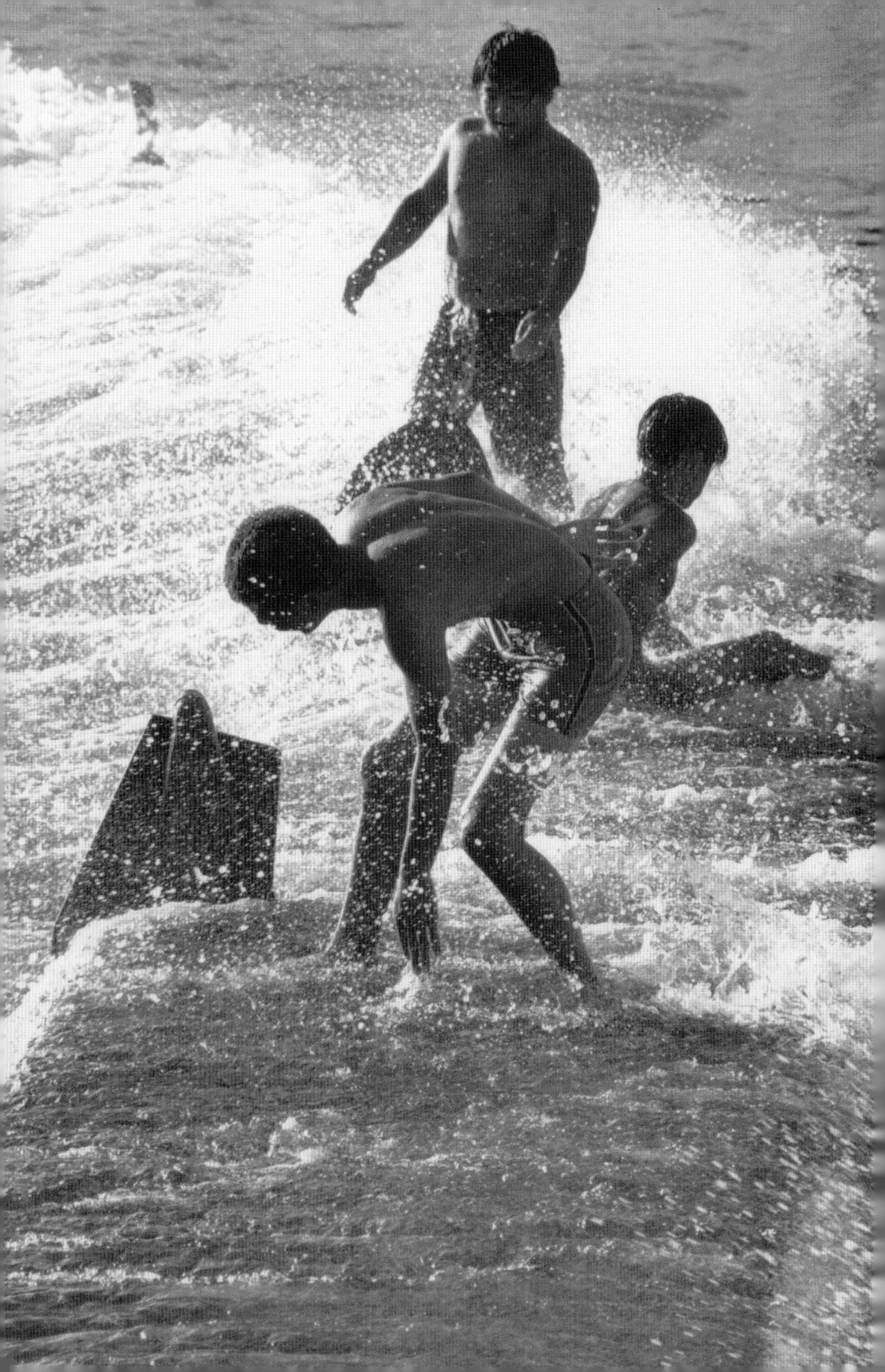

Facing page: Boys scramble for footing atop the super-slippery wall just offshore of Kūhiō Beach at Waikīkī. Note the *paipo* board at left.

This page: Sand sliding (or sand skimming) at Kūhiō Beach around 1962. Young men and boys had been doing this at Waikīkī since at least the late 1940s. Most rides are short and end abruptly, with a fast fall onto the sand—so unlike ocean surfing, the older you get, the less likely you are to take this on.
(Laurence Hata)

[115]

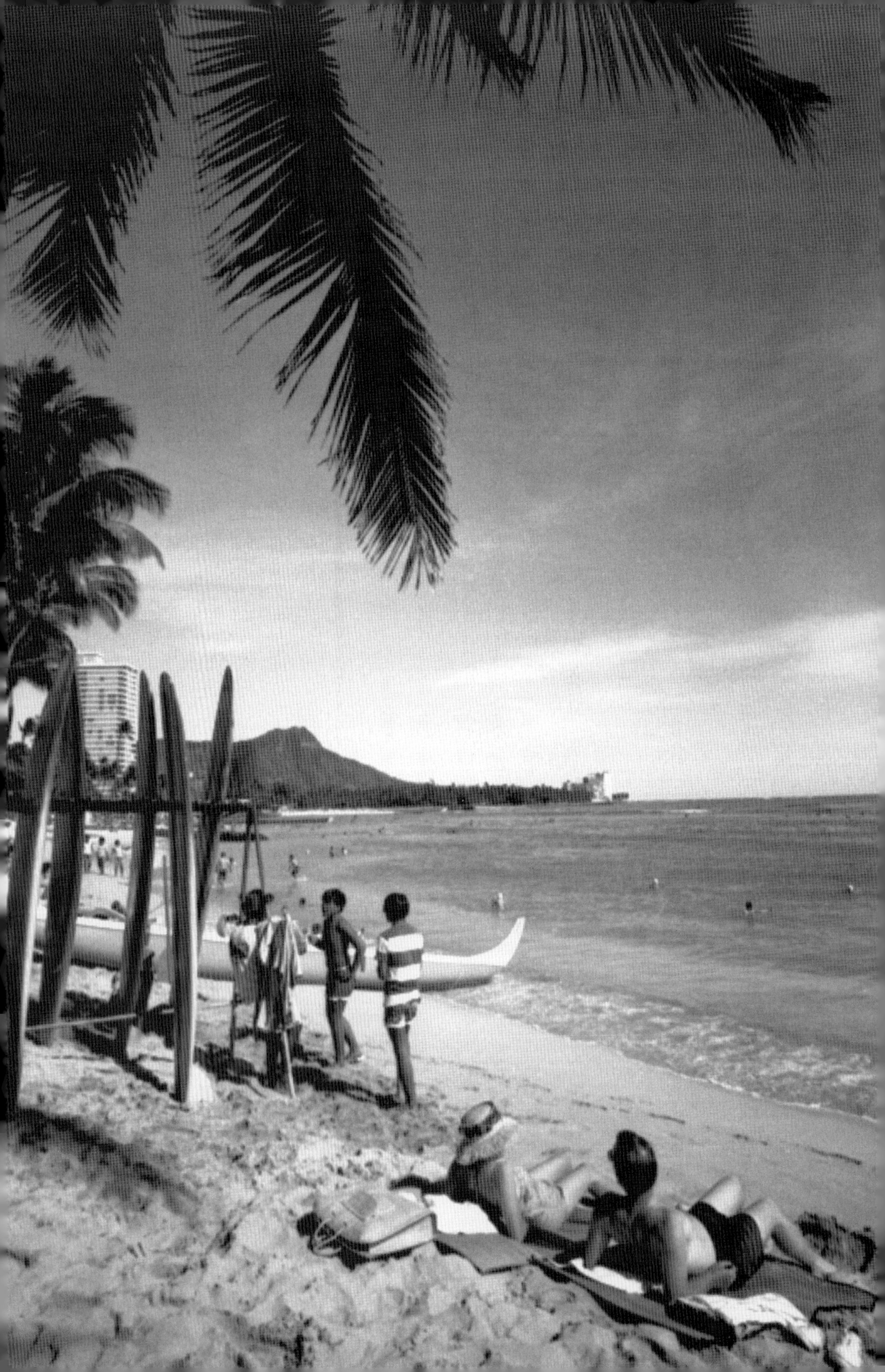

In 1965, surfboards (and canoes) are still very much in evidence on the sands of Waikīkī. *(Laurence Hata)*

Surfing contests had existed as early as 1918, but ran sporadically or without much influence until the International Surfing Championships at Mākaha began in 1954. Although it wasn't evident at the time, the event would point the direction that surfing would eventually go. For in the future, the sport that once was known only to a few would become truly international, and would spawn many more competitions, to be won by celebrity surf stars who could look to earning real money though commercial endorsements. None of this could be foreseen as the first small competitive steps were taken.

This page, above: Even by 1959, a good-sized crowd of over 10,000 gathered on the beach at Mākaha for the yearly surfing contest. *(Robert Butterfield, Laurence Hata Collection)*

Right & facing page: Competitors in numbered jerseys (to aid the judges) show their moves at various Mākaha competitions in the early to middle 1960s. *(Laurence Hata)*

118]

119

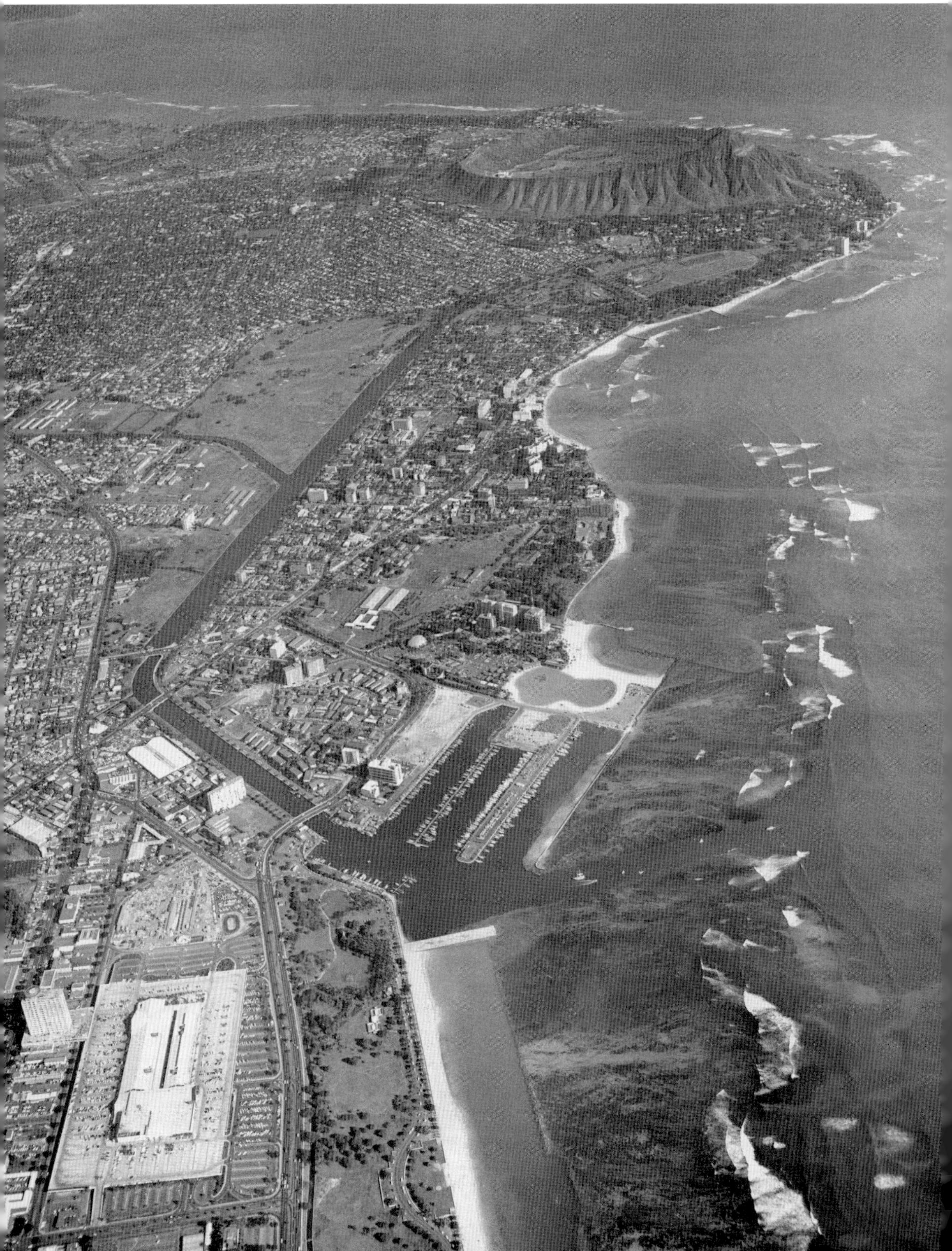

Facing page: From a high vantage point, the surf along Oʻahu's south shore from Ala Moana up around Diamond Head past Kāhala is clearly visible. Also visible, especially at the bottom, are the man-made alterations to the same coastline, where dredging has permanently changed thousands of years of coral growth and the resulting wave patterns. And more alterations would come after this picture was taken in 1961, notably the construction of Magic Island at the entrance to the Ala Wai Boat Harbor. This event would spur the movement to protect surf sites through politics and protest. Whatever is done by humans, however, the surf will not cease. *(Laurence Hata Collection)*
Above: Although shot at Waikīkī in 1968, this image could almost be timeless. *(Hawaii Visitors Bureau, Bank of Hawaii Collection)*

DUKE

Duke Paoa Kahanamoku's life ended in 1968, but amazingly, his fame throughout the world has continued to grow as the sport of surfing grows. There are many reasons why his memory should be honored: He was an extraordinary, natural athlete; he traveled the world as a sportsman and celebrity; he served as the instigator for surfing in Australia and was significant in its beginnings in California; and (not unimportantly) he often looked very good in photos, which made him recognizable everywhere. Duke achieved many things, but it is as the father of surfing that he's best remembered.

Bishop Museum Archives is fortunate to have the largest collection of photographs of Duke Kahanamoku. This is mostly thanks to the generous donations and bequests of his widow, Nadine. On the following pages are examples from this outstanding group of images of the world's most famous surfer.

Facing page: This classic view of Duke Kahanamoku splashing ashore was taken around 1935 for the Pan-Pacific Press Bureau by Nate Farbman. *(N. R. Farbman)*

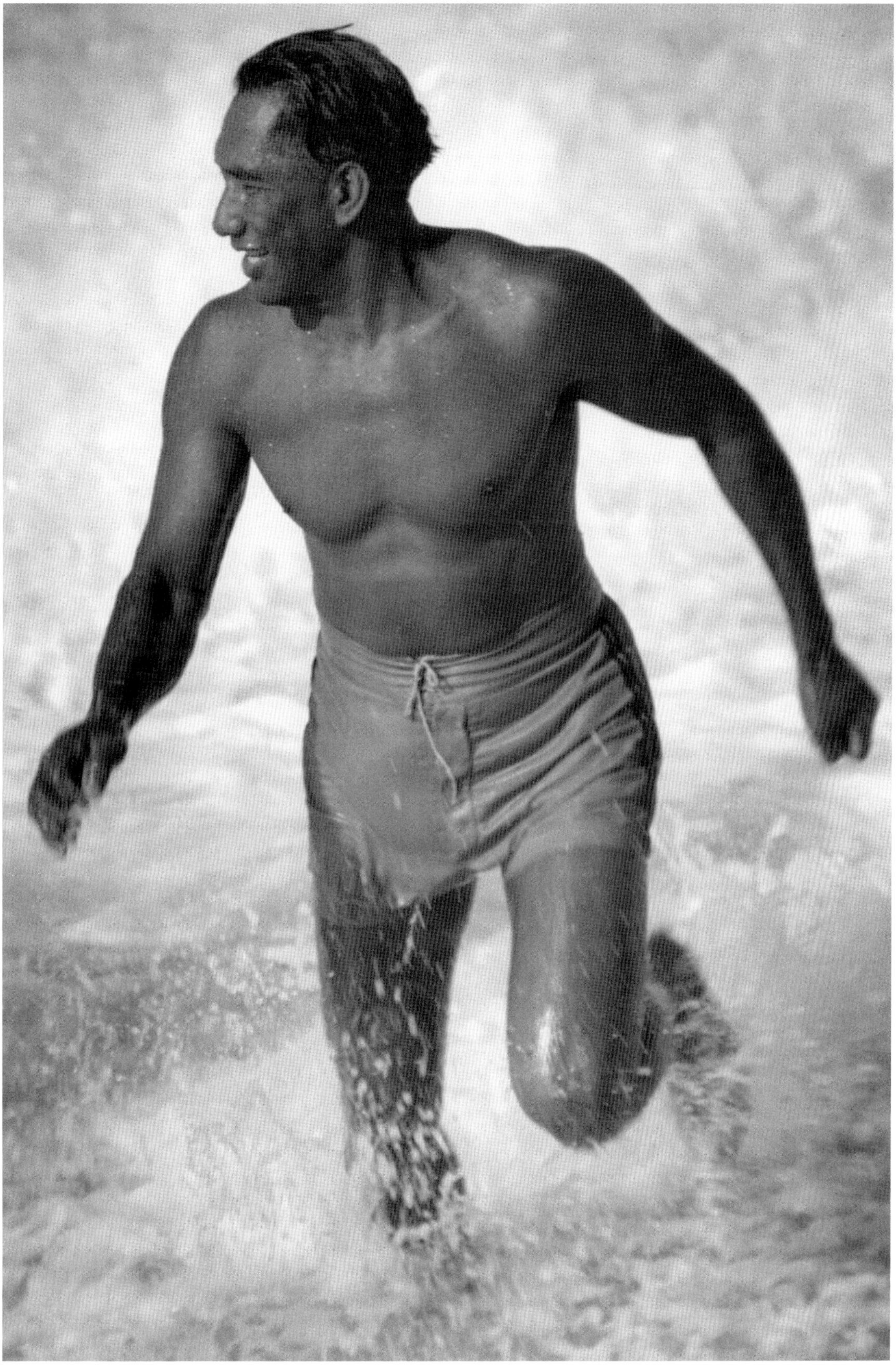

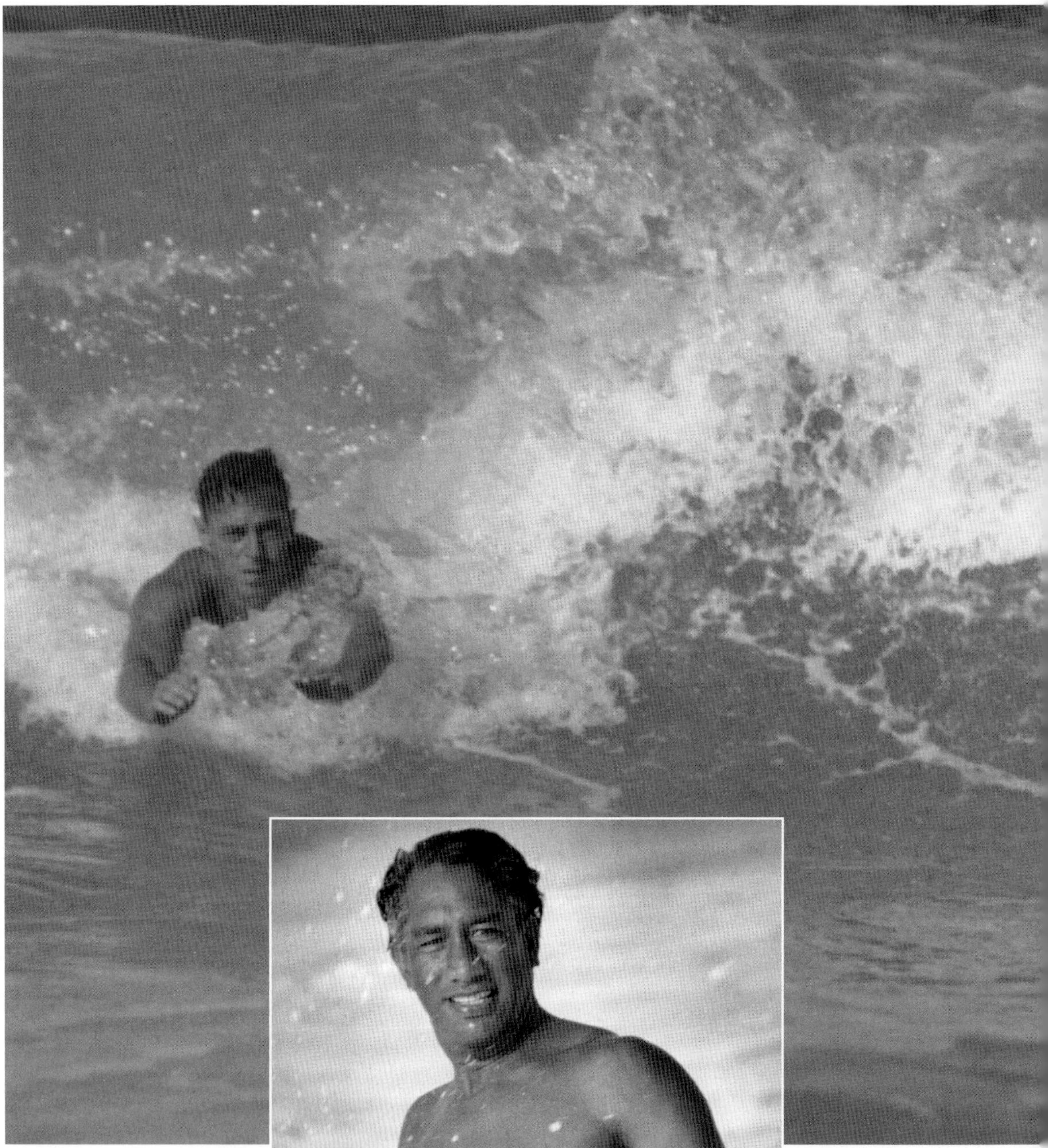

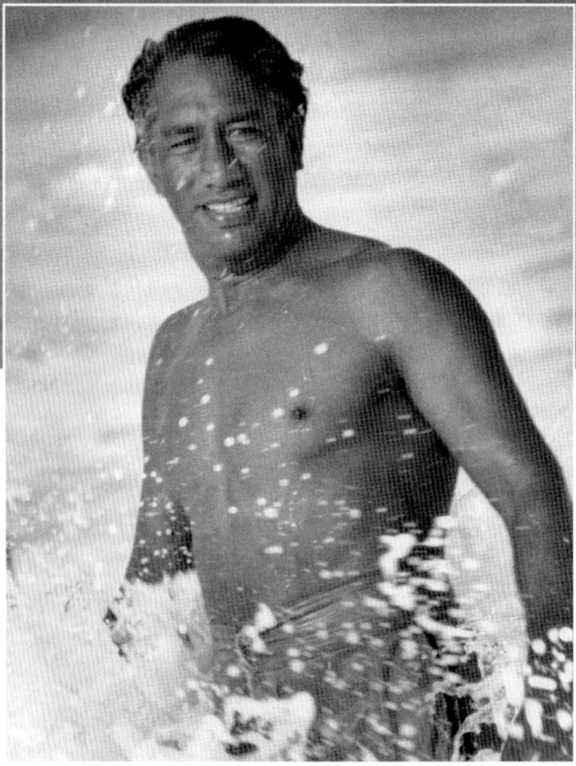

Nathaniel Farbman was a professional photographer who lived in Hawai'i only during the years 1934 to 1937. During this short time he shot hundreds of images with no conscious thought of creating art; instead, his role was to publicize the Hawaiian Islands for strictly commercial reasons. Yet even within these restrictions, Farbman's innate eye and expertise shone through in his composition, lighting, and cropping. His work impresses even today, possibly even more so when it is considered that he often used large cameras that required bulky wooden tripods even in difficult outdoor settings.

A large collection of Nate Farbman's work from his years in Hawai'i was donated to Bishop Museum after his death.

Both pages: Two more admirable studies of Duke, taken in the same session by Farbman. The bodysurfing image, which has deservedly been printed many times, is usually cropped to exclude the man on the left. *(N. R. Farbman)*

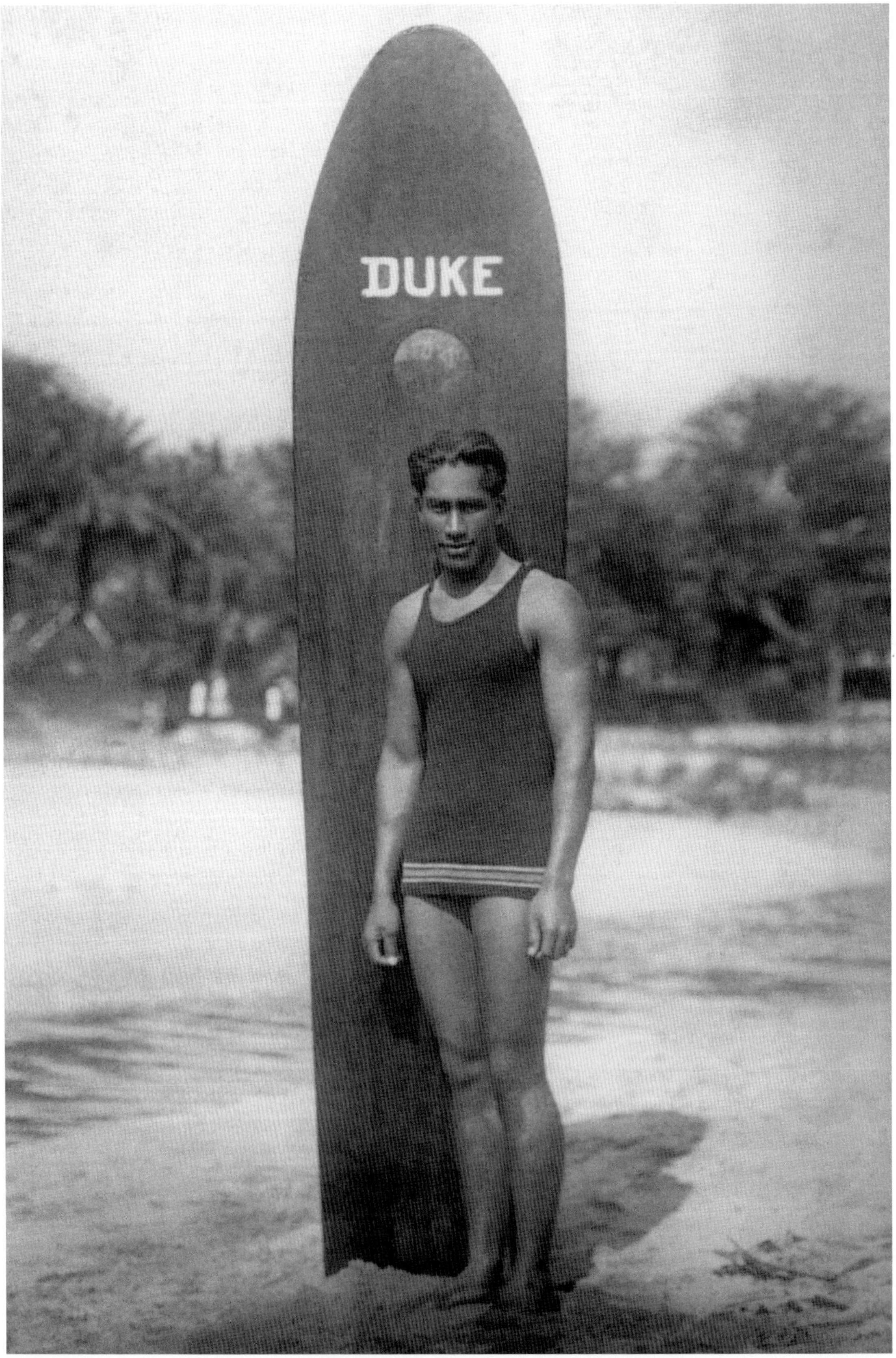
DUKE

It's fitting that Duke Kahanamoku often posed with a surfboard. And from a photographer's standpoint, the board itself makes a good backdrop for a strong vertical composition.

Facing page: A well-known early picture of Duke which was published in a number of different versions, including as a postcard, that probably dates from around 1912. It appears to have been taken next to 'Āpuakēhau Stream in Waikīkī, which at that time ran between the Moana Hotel and the original location of the Outrigger Canoe Club.

This page, above: Duke about twenty years later, posed with a similar but larger surfboard which was made around 1910. This 10-foot board is made of redwood, weighs 70 pounds, and survives today in the Bishop Museum collection. (The handwritten caption at the bottom of the image is by Nadine Kahanamoku.) **Below:** Duke with his 16-foot hollow board, which he built in 1930 following the lead of Tom Blake, who first worked with this style in 1929. The great reduction in weight was crucial in being able to make surfboards of such length. *(Tai Sing Loo)*

This photo, which belonged to Duke personally, is one-of-a-kind because it bears both his autograph and that of Tom Blake. But perhaps even more significant is the surfboard which Tom is holding between them. It's the first one to carry his invention of 1935, the skeg. Time would show this to be a major innovation in advancing the maneuverability of any surfboard. The skeg stands as yet another accomplishment of many for the talented Tom Blake.

While there are thousands of photographs of Duke, comparatively few show him actually engaged in surfing. Here's one, taken by A. R. Gurrey, Jr., probably between 1910 and 1915. Gurrey is well-regarded by historians and collectors for his booklet entitled *The Surf Riders of Hawaii*, one of the first publications (if not the first) exclusively about surfing, in this same period. *(A. R. Gurrey, Jr.)*

Tandem surfing requires a large, steady board and an experienced (and strong) man on the bottom. Duke was more than capable of handling the necessary duties, as these photos prove.

Above: Aquaplaning was a predecessor to waterskiing; it utilized a single, wide board instead of two separate skis. In this picture, Harold Castle (who grew up in Waikīkī in his family's palatial mansion) stands on the shoulders of his friend Duke, who holds the tow rope from the motor boat. It's a daring display, and both men looked pleased to have achieved it. In the background, on the far right, the Moana Hotel is in the process of being enlarged. The year is 1917.

Above: Duke (or perhaps his brother Sam) carries Jane Waite on his shoulders in the Waikīkī surf in 1929. Three years later, a national magazine *(Liberty)* printed this happy photo with a caption that disapproved of such cross-racial interactions: "A white girl riding with a 'surf-board god' - that is, a Kanaka instructor." The tone of the article it accompanied is clear from its title: "A Paradise Gone Mad - Facing The Facts In Hawaii." *(Warren Tong)*

Following pages: A gag picture taken at Long Beach, California in the 1920s, when Duke spent time on the west coast. He was undeniably an outstanding sports talent, but even the great Duke Kahanamoku could not play golf while surfing.

[131]

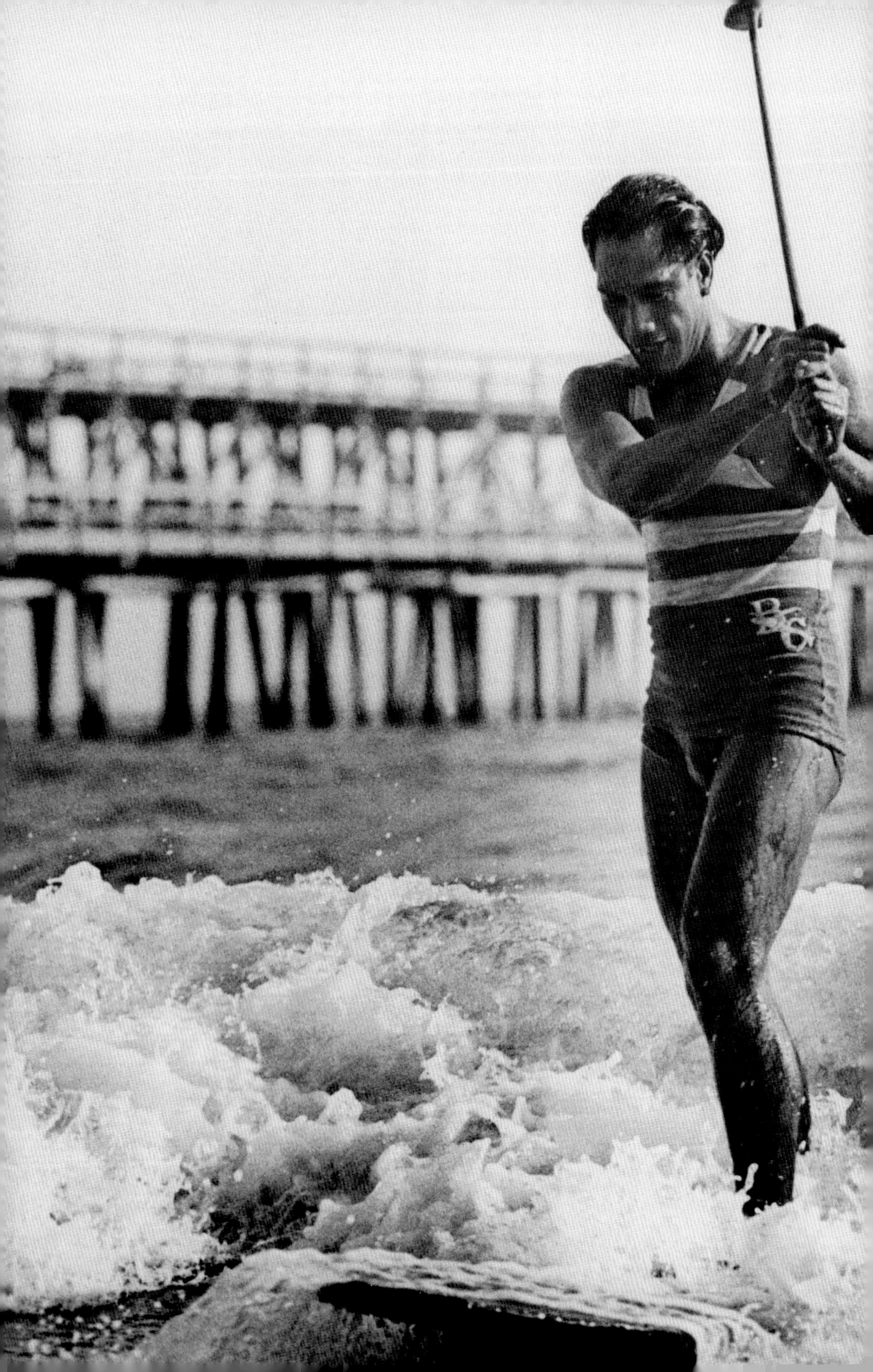

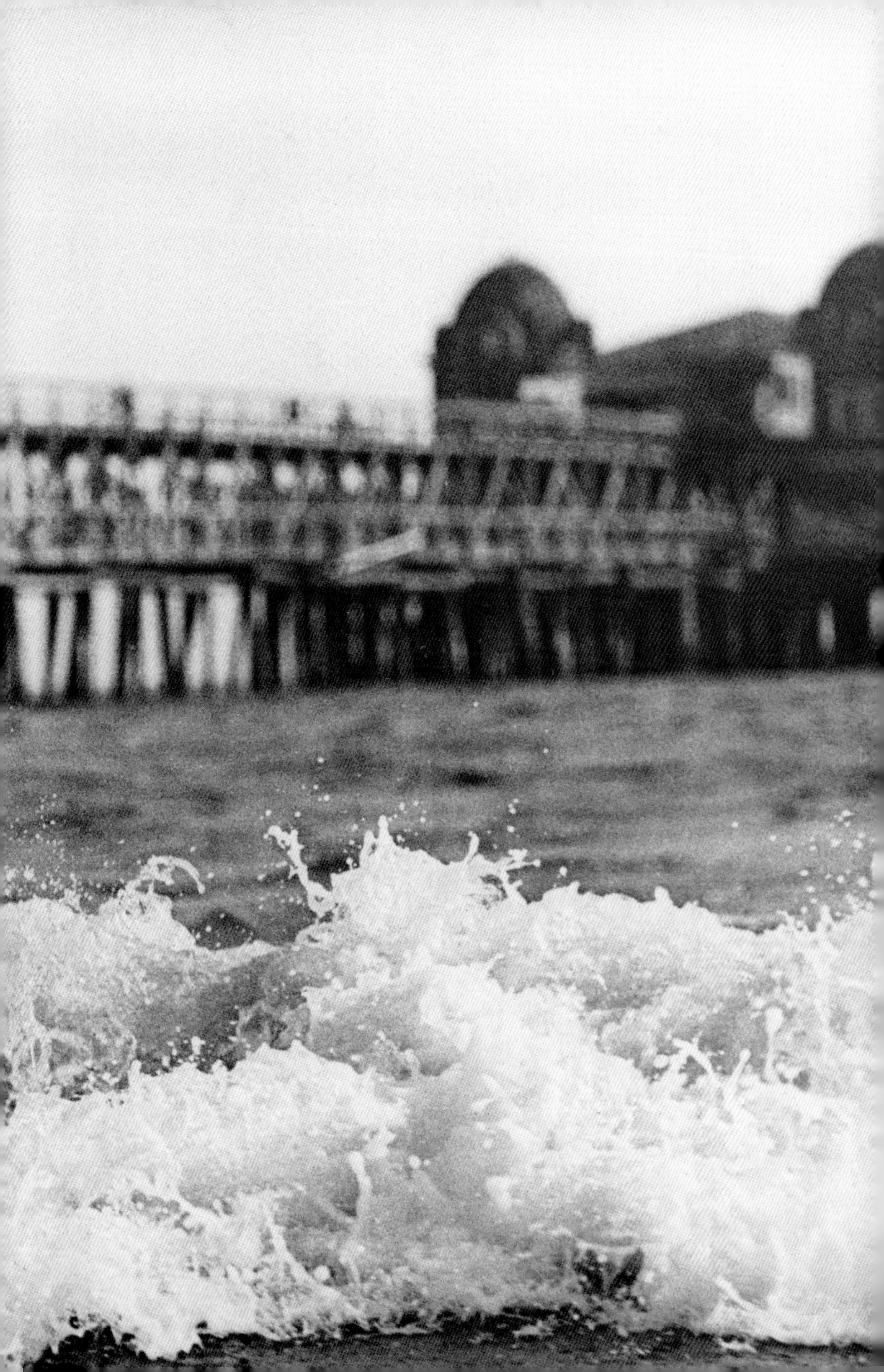

One of Duke's best-remembered accomplishments was the popularizing of surfing in Australia. Before his visit there, the ocean was regarded with a mixture of desire and fear, with the beginnings of the organized lifesaving that would become a feature of Australian beaches. Bodysurfing was already established and other scattered attempts had been made to interact with waves, but for the most part people were discouraged (or prohibited) from doing anything too daring. Duke knocked aside any of these hesitations with his marvelous displays of surfing skill. From December 1914 through February 1915 (which was, of course, the middle of summer in the southern hemisphere), he performed numerous swimming and surfing demonstrations to widespread excitement. He brought no surfboard with him on his journey; as many as three were made on location for his use, and he per-

VISIT TO FRESHWATER, JANUARY, 1915
by DUKE POA KAHANAMOKU....

sonally did the finishing work on at least the first one. In decades to come, surfing in Australia would become tremendously popular and would produce international champions—thanks to Duke's initial appearance.

Facing page: The master makes it all look quite effortless at Freshwater Beach, New South Wales.

Above: Enthralled admirers surround Duke at Freshwater in January 1915. His first public surfing demonstration had occurred here a short time earlier on December 23, 1914. The hand-lettered caption at the top of the picture misspells Duke's middle name, which was actually "Paoa."

[135]

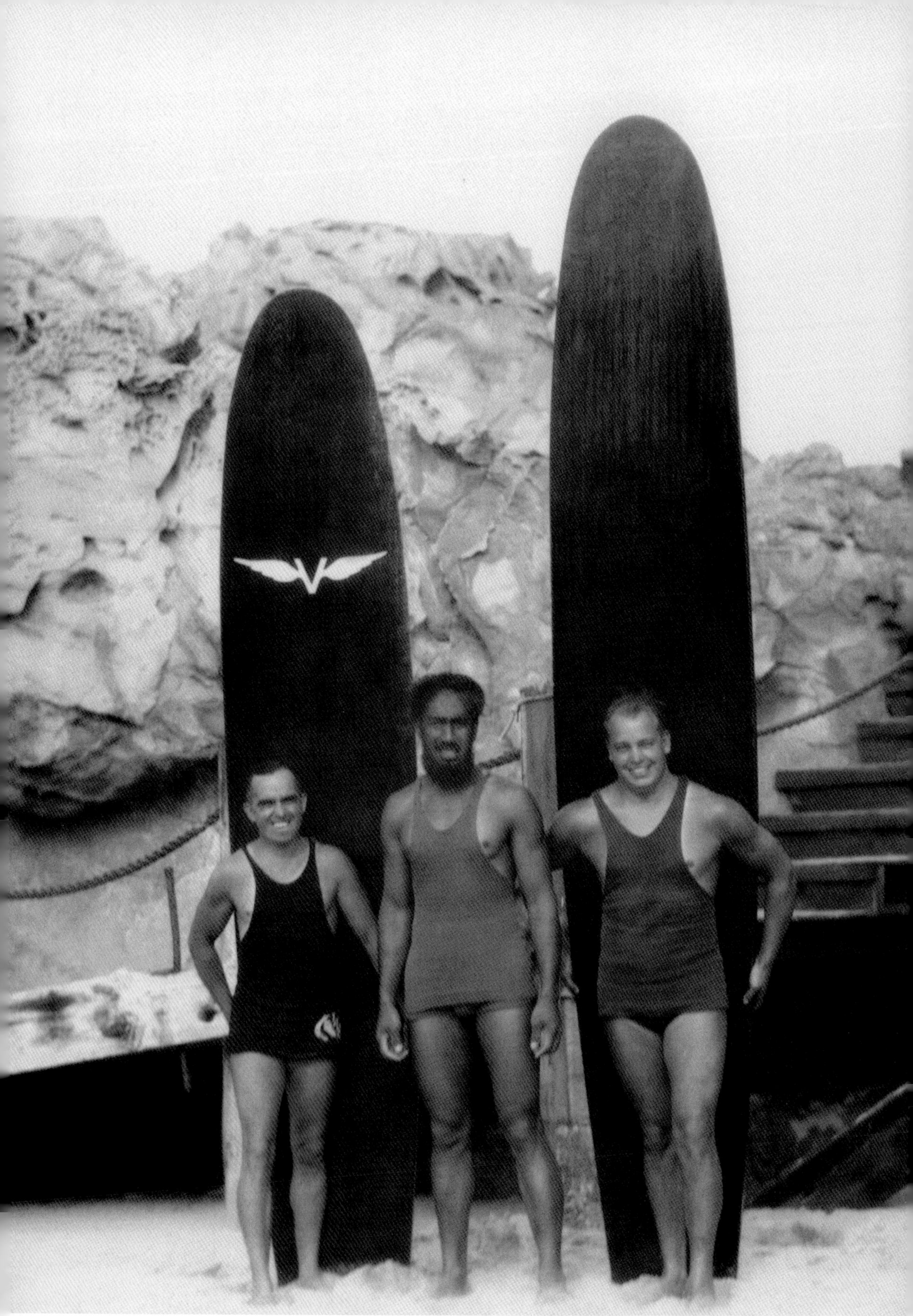

From about 1922 to 1929, Duke lived mostly in Southern California. In addition to working as a lifeguard for a time at the Santa Monica Beach Club in 1925, he also made a number of movie appearances in various small roles.

Facing page: A heavy beard gives Duke an unusual appearance in this pose on a California beach. The facial hair was grown for a film part.

Above: Fellow watermen line up for a picture with the 57-year-old Duke at San Onofre in California in August 1948. The photographer, Doc Ball (or John Heath Ball, a dentist in real life, but an avid surfer as well), was the premier surf photographer in the area, who thoroughly documented the sport starting in the 1930s. *(Doc Ball)*

As a well-known personality, Duke had to interact with the media for much of his life, though he undoubtedly would have preferred to avoid most of the attention.

Above: With oversized microphone in hand, Duke says a few words to the national audience of the famous *Hawaii Calls* radio show in the middle 1930s. The program's host, Webley Edwards, is ready on the right to take over the announcing duties. It appears Edwards is about to embark on a canoe ride in Waikīkī's surf, which he most likely would describe on the air as it occurred. Could the presence of musician Alvin Isaacs (holding guitar in the background on the right) mean that there would be live music accompanying the description? *(N. R. Farbman)*

In 1957, Duke was the subject of an episode of *This Is Your Life*, an NBC television show in which celebrities were brought together with various people who they had known in the past, for a recap of their life experiences. The program's gimmick was that the stars never knew beforehand that they were going to appear, and the guests were always a surprise (pleasant, it was hoped). On the set in Burbank, Duke was greeted by (among others) his wife, his siblings, his old swimming competitor Johnny Weismuller (later a movie actor), and three survivors of a boat sinking who he had saved from drowning in 1925. The host, Ralph Edwards, autographed this photo to him personally.

[139]

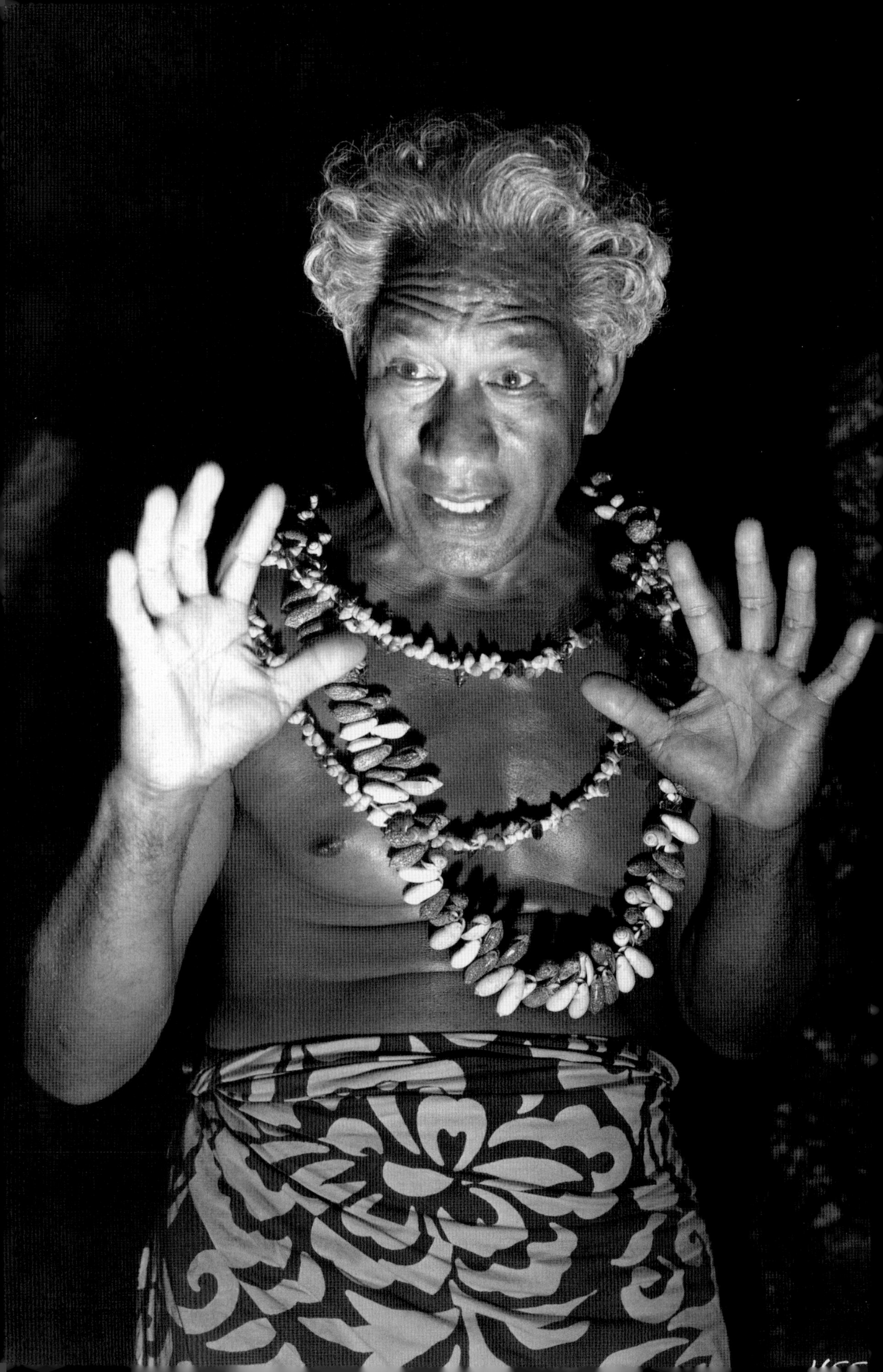

Duke goes Hollywood! Glimpses of his many film roles, in a variety of ethnic guises, include *(facing page)* an apprehensive pose at the edge of a glowing South Sea lava pit (*Wake of the Red Witch*, 1948), and *(this page, clockwise from top)* a Pacific Islander (1927), probably a "Persian guard" (*Woman Wise*, 1928), a pirate (*Old Ironsides*, 1927), and a Sioux chief (*The Pony Express*, 1925). Nearly all of Duke's films were made in the 1920s, and although he hobnobbed socially with various movie stars, his parts were small. A great many films from this period have been permanently lost, so most of Duke's appearances can never be seen again.

[141]

Famous in his own right, Duke played the role of a ceremonial greeter from the 1920s into the 1960s. Here are a few of the Hollywood stars with whom he interacted: Cary Grant *(above)* and Shirley Temple *(right)* in the 1930s, and Richard Boone and Peter Lawford in the early 1950s *(facing page)*.

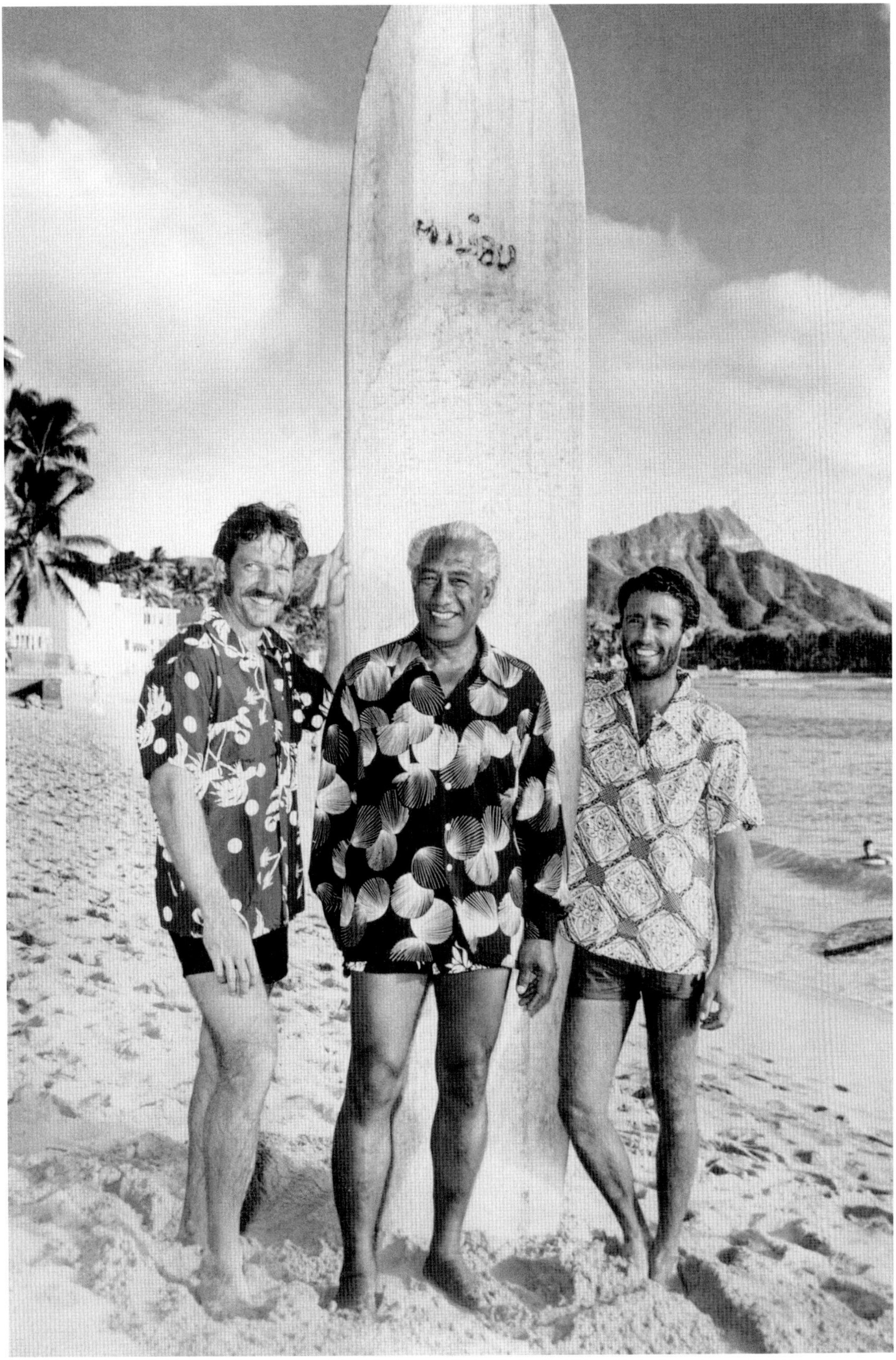

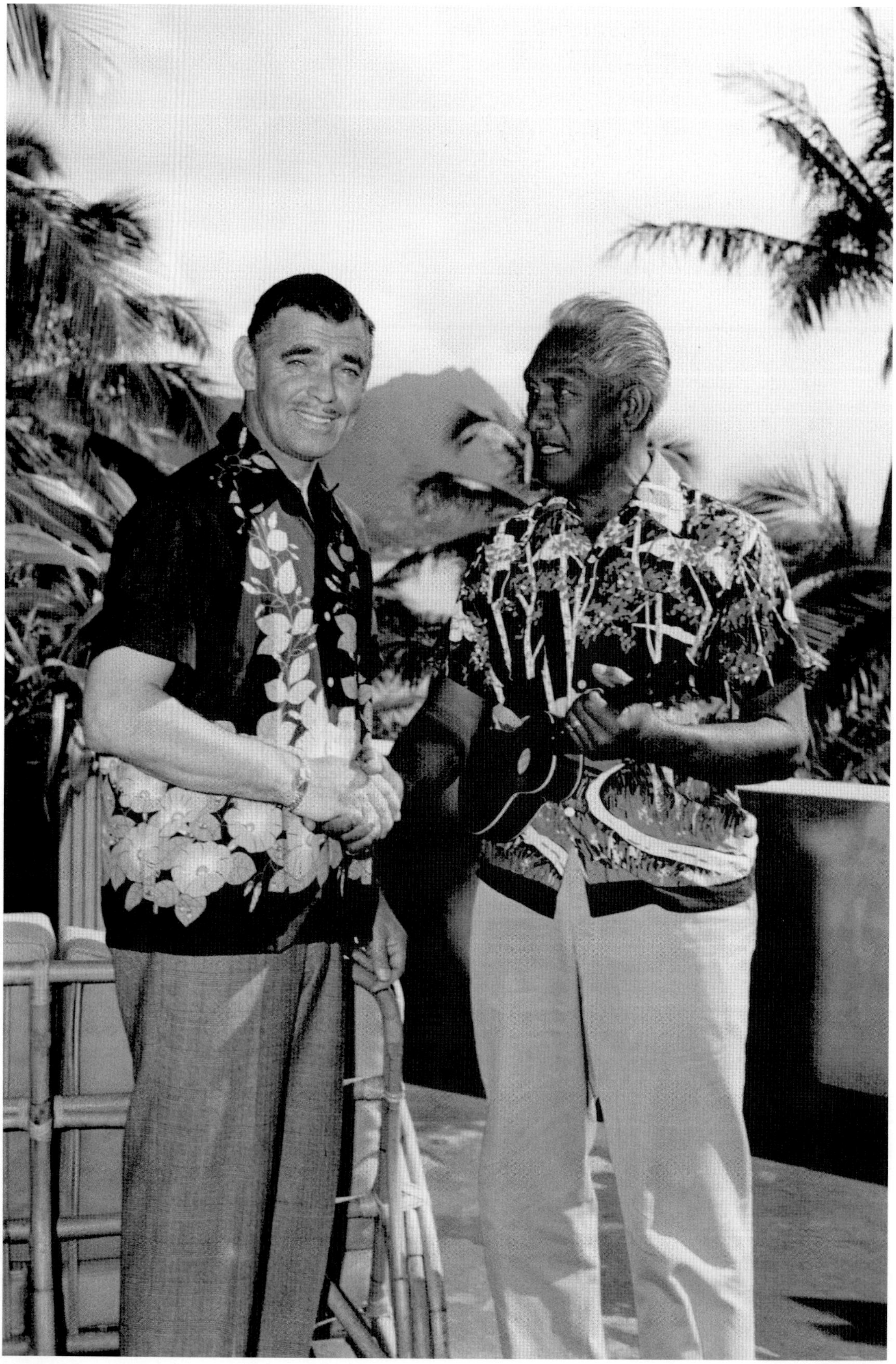

Facing page: In 1950, Duke licensed his name to a mainland clothing manufacturer for the marketing of Duke Kahanamoku-brand aloha shirts. For several years afterwards, various visiting male celebrities posed for publicity shots with Duke while wearing one of his shirts. One of them was Clark Gable, seen here.

This page: Other notables to enjoy Duke's company while in Honolulu were baseball legend Babe Ruth in 1933 or 1934 *(left)* and famous aviator Amelia Earhart in 1935 *(below)*, who snacks on a tasty pineapple. *(Below: N. R. Farbman)*

Above: When Duke met Duke: In Hollywood for the filming of *Wake of the Red Witch*, Duke Kahanamoku demonstrated the use of a throw net to his costar John Wayne (who signed this photograph with his nickname, Duke) and associate producer Edmund Grainger. "Son of Taro Tato," also inscribed here by Wayne, was the name his character was known by on the island ruled by the native chief, played by Duke.

Facing page: In the 1930s, Duke was filmed at Bishop Museum dressed in authentic ancient Hawaiian royal attire from the Museum's collection. On the right is the Museum's director, Dr. Peter Buck. The re-enactment was probably staged for one of the *Fitzpatrick Travel Talks*, a series of travelogues released by MGM to movie theaters internationally.

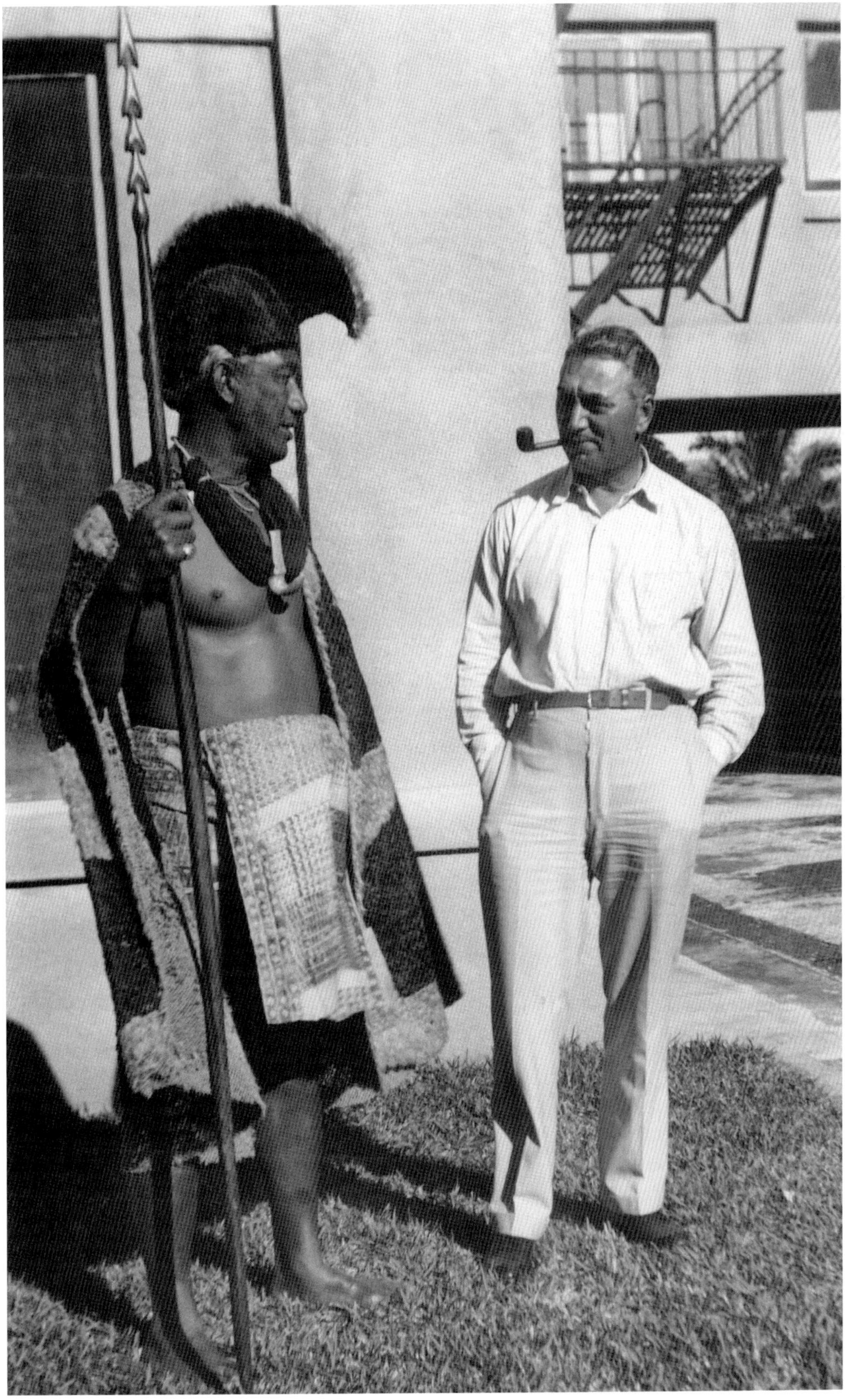

Above: Duke cuts loose on the dance floor of the Royal Hawaiian Hotel with professional hula dancer Aggie Auld in the middle 1930s. Auld was known for introducing the cellophane hula skirt to Hawai'i in that decade, which she's wearing in this picture. *(N. R. Farbman)* **Right:** On a visit to San Francisco in the 1940s, Duke posed for a gag souvenir photo as a strong man lifting 1,000 pounds.

Facing page: Duke owned many cars in his lifetime and had his picture taken with a number of them. Here he admires the decorative surfer on his new 1955 Imperial, at the Universal Motors showroom in Honolulu. Hood ornaments of this (or similar) design had been available from at least 1917, and all of Duke's later automobiles sported surfers like this until his death.

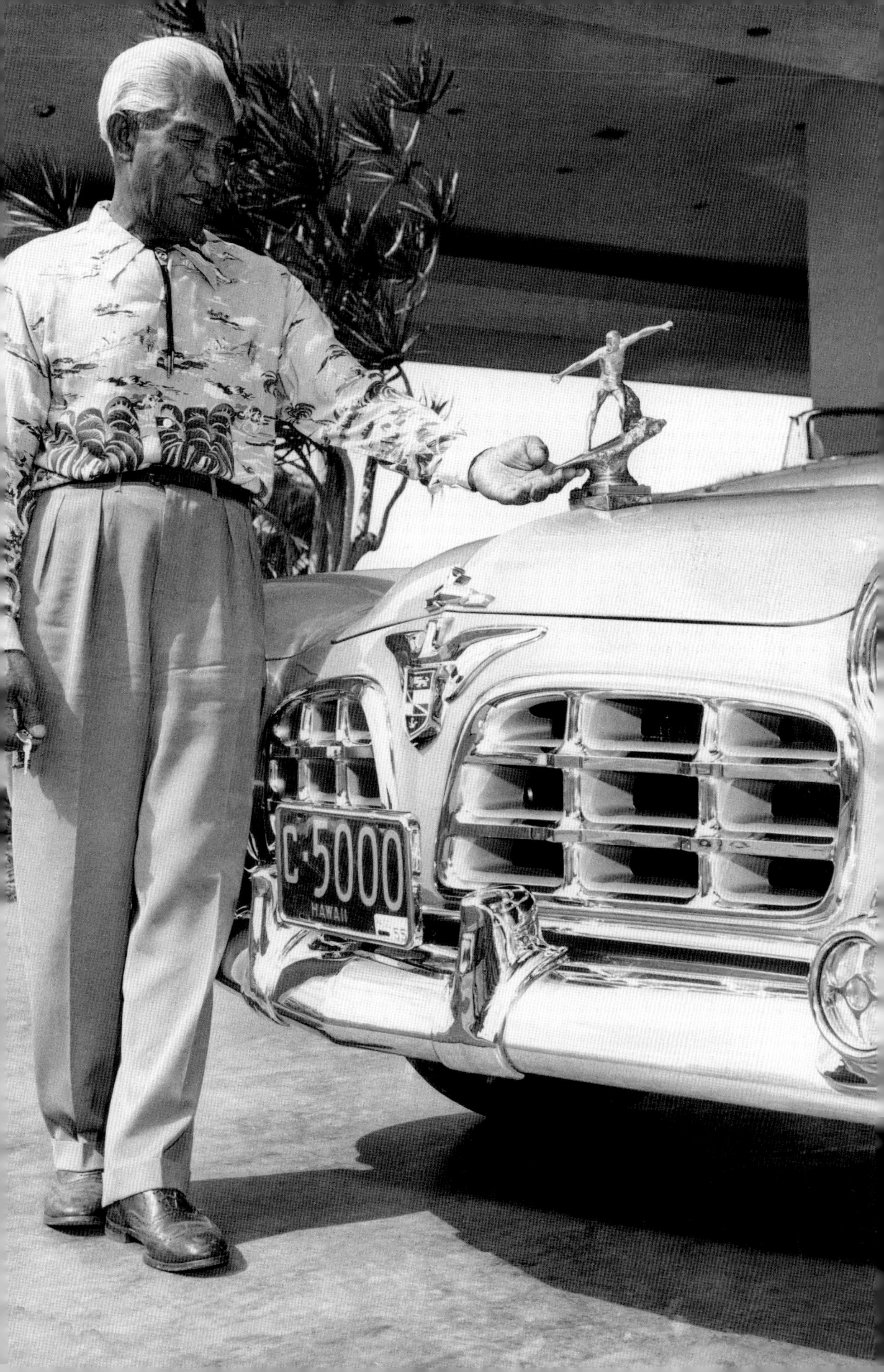
C-5000
HAWAII
55

Fishing Party

There was a great deal of glamour and excitement in Duke's life, but he was probably happiest when he was able to do the traditional Hawaiian things that he'd grown up with. After his low-key wedding in Kona in August 1940, Duke and his bride Nadine had their honeymoon at the beach house of his best man, Francis H. I. Brown. The setting was beautifully rustic, with simple accommodations, and Duke could take it easy as much as he wished.

Facing page: The successful end of a spearfishing session, with Duke's brother Sam included in the center.

Above: Nadine took this playful snapshot of her new husband skinny-dipping in a brackish water natural pool in the ʻaʻā lava. This looks like more fun than having to greet yet another arriving movie star or politician.

Duke relaxes with a "men's adventure" magazine, popular in the 1950s and '60s. These told action-packed "he-man" stories—supposedly true—of spy intrigues, wild animal attacks, violent wartime battles, and dangerously sexy dames. Duke Kahanamoku's real life may have lacked these elements, but it was no less active or amazing than the fictional ones he's reading about here. No magazine story could top the experiences this great man had actually lived.

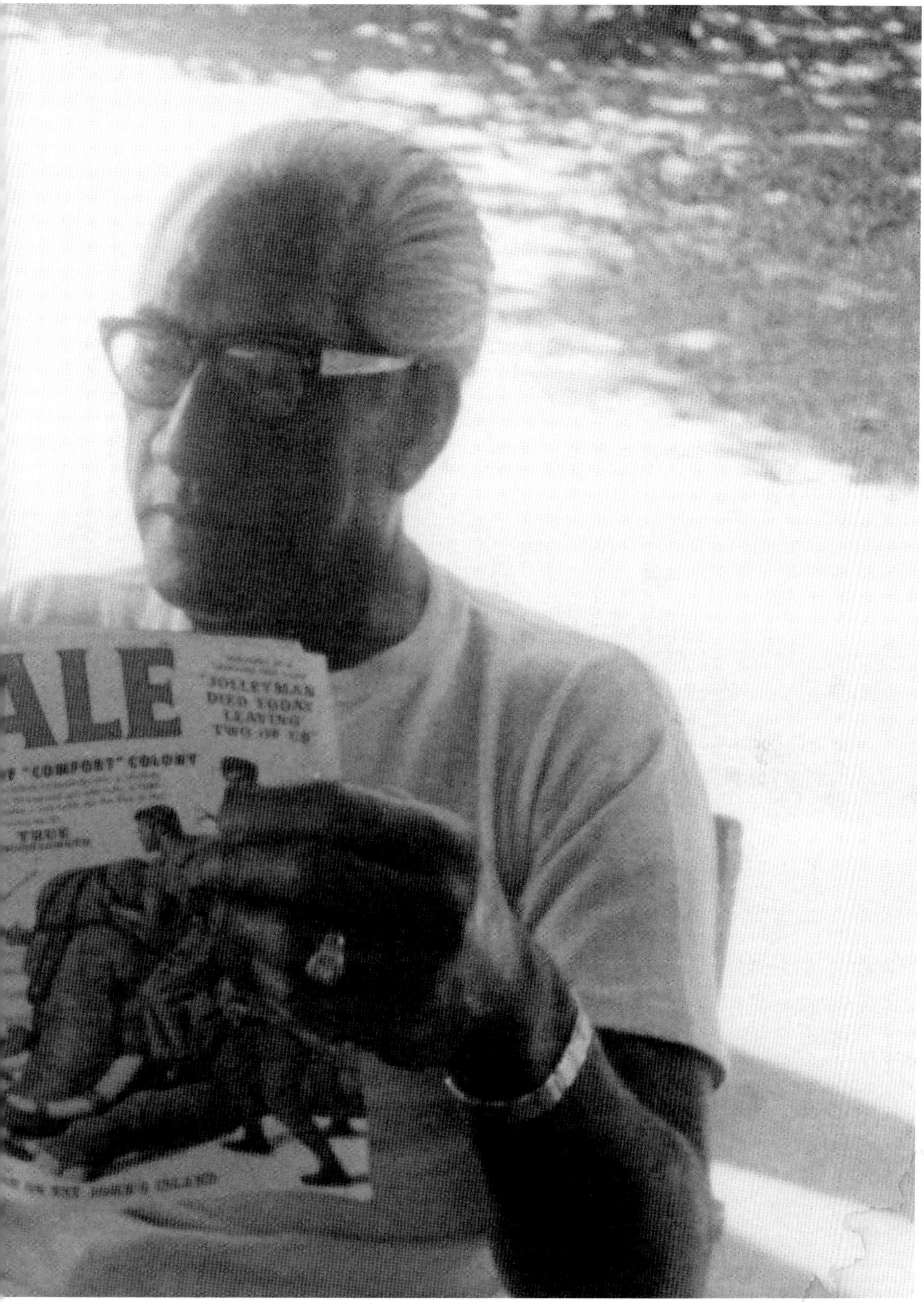
ALE
"JOLLEYMAN DIED TODAY LEAVING TWO OF US"
"COMFORT" COLONY

The end of a ride on a Waikīkī wave. *(Ray Jerome Baker)*

All the photographs in this book are from Bishop Museum Archives, which holds the largest historic photo collection in Hawai'i. Visit the Bishop Museum website (www.bishopmuseum.org) for more information on these treasures and how you can see them in person, and order copies.